Peter's Principles

learning to follow Jesus

Peter's Principles

learning to follow Jesus

Glenn Parkinson

GrowthGround
Kindle Direct Publishing

Cover design by Micki Parkinson

ISBN: 979-8-9884662-0-8

Dedication

To my grandsons, Matthew and Mark.
May Christ's first disciple guide you in following Jesus.

Contents

Acknowledgments

My previous books were reworked versions of sermon series. This is my first effort to put together a book from scratch. It's allowed me to involve many others in the project, and I'm grateful to them all.

Two study groups spent several months interacting over the draft material: the Peter's Principles Sunday morning adult class at Severna Park Evangelical Presbyterian and a long-running men's study meeting at our mother church in Annapolis. Thank you for trusting that I had something worthwhile to say and helping me make sense of it.

Vivian Sockett graciously helped me to be accessible and engaging. If you find the book to be either of those things, know that she had something to do with it.

Julie Soltis led prayer for God's blessing upon this project and where it goes from here. Her faith is infectious, and I believe God heard and answered her.

Rebecca Reed graciously and patiently edited my writing. She knew just what needed attention while encouraging me at the same time. The book was always better after she worked with it.

I am especially thankful for a group of brothers I meet with weekly. The core includes Graham Gutsche, Stuart Caton, Bruce Holtzman, and Frank Rouland. They reviewed each chapter and were constant sources of insightful feedback, wisdom, and enthusiasm.

And thanks to Micki, the love of my life, who always points me to Jesus and confidently urges me to stop beating around the bush and say what I mean. Anyone who knows me knows she is always part of the best I have to give.

Introduction

If anyone serves me, he must follow me. (John 12:26)

What does it mean to follow Jesus?

American society has never been less interested in following anyone associated with traditional or institutional authority, instead preferring to fly in the swirling winds of secular culture. Those winds take society in directions that treat a biblical perspective as irrelevant, incomprehensible, or dangerous. Social pressure demands the freedom to create identities unfettered by civil constraints. This is a powerful force in politics, entertainment, and education. The search for one's authentic self is the quest of the 21st century.

What a golden opportunity for Christians to put forward the alternative of following Jesus. For 2,000 years, millions from every culture have found life in the Son of God. People are no more lost today than in any other generation. Followers of Jesus do not need to change their culture before they can represent Christ faithfully and effectively. The reverse is often true: cultures change as Christ draws people to the Living God.

But are today's Christians clear about what it means to follow Jesus? The Church is caught up in the overall decline of confidence in institutional authority. Scandals involving evangelical leaders paint the gospel message as insincere and

1

believers as gullible. Religious voices suggest that faith is incompatible with science. In America, biblical theology has never been more neglected. And none of us are immune to society's strong current that presses us to abandon biblical paths for excursions mapped to our preferences. Cracks in the Christian faith are readily filled by polarized politics, forcing the fractures even wider. This perfect storm has left Christians with traditions they are no longer willing to defend, leaders they no longer trust, and theology they no longer understand. The trend to deconstruct Christian faith is prone to throw out the baby with the bathwater. The word evangelical and even the term Christian is becoming detached from Christ and his Church altogether, mere labels in a culture war that has us attacking anything that moves.

The need of the hour

One way to recapture what it means to follow Jesus is to revisit the original term that defined the followers of Christ: "And in Antioch the disciples were first called Christians" (Acts 11:26). Before the followers of Jesus were called Christians, they were known as disciples.

A disciple is a spiritual apprentice. Apprentices learn by studying under and working alongside masters in a field. A Christian disciple learns how to follow Jesus from Christians already doing so. Then, like any other apprentice, Christians spend the rest of their lives practicing and perfecting what they originally learned. In practice, a *disciple* is another term for a Christian, and *discipleship* refers to an initial period of training that prepares Christians to follow Jesus throughout their lives.

There are many discipleship programs. While they only reach a small fraction of believers, they represent some of the best Christian training available. As a Pastor with forty-four years of service, I've used and benefitted from several. Yet despite that, Christians seem increasingly confused about what it means to follow Jesus. And if we are confused, how can we meaningfully invite others to join us? We need something in addition to what we already have.

Before becoming a pastor, my passion and undergraduate degree were in physics. I learned that to build something that works well—an experiment, an apparatus, a computer simulation—you have to begin by understanding the underlying dynamics of what you are working with. Good construction techniques are essential but not enough. You must also understand how related forces interact and work together most efficiently. You might build an airplane without a good understanding of aerodynamics, but you won't make a good airplane regardless of how excellent your tools are. Likewise, you could design a car without a working knowledge of fuel efficiency, but why would you want to? It's easy to use good tools to make something; it's harder to make something that works well.

Most discipleship studies focus on tools—spiritual disciplines like prayer, Bible study, meditation, care for the poor, and many others. I will not deal with any of those things in depth. This is partly because others have done so quite well and partly because we need something more. We need to understand *how discipleship works*. Spiritual disciplines and tools are like good driving habits—essential when driving a car. But if today's discipleship were a car, it would be broken down and on the side of the road. Good driving habits don't help when the car doesn't work and you are forced to hitchhike through life with whatever traffic is moving by.

Help from someone who knows

We will always need good training in how to pray, evangelize, meditate, and all the rest. But right now, we also need a sense of how the process of following Jesus is supposed to work—what it's supposed to accomplish and how its different pieces interact most effectively. Is there an approach that will consistently yield good results? Is such an approach taught in God's Word?

The answer is yes. The principles are not hidden in an obscure passage but are clearly labeled and literally listed by the first Christian disciple.

3

This book consists of three sections. The first introduces us to Peter and gives an overview of the remarkable text we will be studying. The second looks at Peter's growth in seven qualities and how they summarize the basic training every Christian needs. Finally, the third section suggests conclusions that could change our practice of discipleship and might also change our outcomes.

I've included discussion questions to facilitate personal reflection and group interaction. I hope you enjoy the journey.

Overview

2 Peter 1:3-8

Chapter 1: The First Christian Disciple

I tell you, you are Peter, and on this rock I will build my church. (Matthew 16:18)

This is a study of Christian discipleship. It is based on the teaching and experience of the Apostle Peter because Simon Peter was Jesus' prototype disciple. We know this for two reasons.

First, the early Church Fathers identified him as the source behind the Gospel of Mark, which the other Gospel writers used. He is also the early focus in the Book of Acts as the people of God transitioned from the physical children of Abraham to the spiritual children of Abraham from every nation and race.[1] We see the nature and impact of Jesus' discipleship primarily through Peter's eyes.

Second, there is Peter's name or name change. The traditional Roman Catholic/Protestant discussion of Matthew 16:18 involves whether the rock reference is tied to Peter himself or his confession. Unfortunately, this debate obscures the Old Testament reference that gives the name meaning. So let's begin by setting aside that classic argument from Church history and let the Bible explain why Jesus chose the name he did, what that would mean for Peter, and what it now means for us.

---

[1] Genesis 12:1-3; Galatians 3:7-9.

§

553 BC

The prophet Daniel lay pondering the meaning of what he just saw. Can you even label a vision as something you see? It had appeared inside his head. God had already given him the wisdom to interpret specific dreams and signs, but this was the first time the communication came directly to him. He immediately understood the symbols. They portrayed the theme that had occupied his mind and prayers for fifty years: the coming kingdom of God. It was the grand theme of Abraham, Moses, David, and all the Hebrew Scriptures. God's kingdom had been imperfectly fleshed out in the nation of Israel. But as unfaithful Israel lay defeated by Babylon, Daniel's thoughts increasingly turned to the promised fullness of God's kingdom that would involve all nations.

Daniel had prayed day after day to understand this coming kingdom. He had to. His faith—and sanity—had depended on it. When he was a teenager in Israel, his world was shattered by the mighty armies of Babylon as they crushed the walls of Jerusalem and tore apart God's Temple. He and many others were taken captive to be indoctrinated into Babylonian culture. He lost everything: his family, his name, his heritage, his language, his friends (all but three, who were captives with him), his hopes for wife and family (the servants of Nebuchadnezzar were typically made eunuchs), and his God ...

No, not his God. They could not take away his God. Babylon's victory was not a victory over Israel's Lord. Isaiah and Jeremiah had forewarned that this catastrophe was coming—not despite God's power but because of it. Generations of sin called for severe consequences to awaken God's people. Because the Lord had ordained Israel's defeat, Daniel clung to God's promise to bring Israel back to its land and go on to fulfill his ultimate promise of a forever kingdom drawn from every nation on earth.

Daniel's first glimpse of this kingdom was not from his own vision but from Babylonian King Nebuchadnezzar's remarkable dream fifty years earlier that he had been called to interpret. At the time, Daniel was a young man just out of training in the Babylonian academy for Magi (yes, the same group that much later appeared in the Christmas story). The King dreamed of a massive statue with a head of gold, chest and arms of silver, middle and thighs of bronze, legs of iron, and feet a mixture of iron and clay.[2] God gave Daniel the wisdom to recognize a vertical timeline stretching centuries into the future. The different metals represented a succession of kingdoms. Later visions specified that gold represented Babylon; silver the Medes and Persians; bronze Greece; and iron an empire of unparalleled power, which did not yet exist or have a name but, from our perspective, clearly described Rome. The statue's feet pictured a time toward the end of Rome's dominance when it would divide into parts, still strong but beginning to disintegrate as an Empire.

The statue was a prop for the critical element of the dream: a rock fell from heaven to smash the figure at its disintegrating feet, which chronologically tied its arrival to when future Rome would start to break apart. The statue was shattered, but the rock began to grow. It became a mountain, eventually covering the entire earth—quite a dream.

This is how Daniel interpreted that rock:

> And in the days of those kings the God of heaven will set up a kingdom that shall never be destroyed, nor shall the kingdom be left to another people. It shall break in pieces all these kingdoms and bring them to an end, and it shall stand forever. (Daniel 2:44)

The rock in Nebuchadnezzar's dream was Daniel's first prophetic glimpse of the kingdom of God.

Now, fifty years later, Daniel had a vision of his own. At first, it portrayed a sequence of kingdoms like the sequence in

---

[2] Daniel 2:1-45.

the king's dream. This time, however, there was more detail about the ultimate kingdom that would sweep away all others:

> As I looked, thrones were placed, and the Ancient of Days took his seat; his clothing was white as snow, and the hair of his head like pure wool; his throne was fiery flames; its wheels were burning fire. (Daniel 7:9)

In this vision of God on his throne, Daniel saw the overthrow of all human kingdoms. They were displaced by a new domain represented by an astounding figure:

> I saw in the night visions, and behold, with the clouds of heaven there came one like a son of man, and he came to the Ancient of Days and was presented before him.
> And to him was given dominion and glory and a kingdom, that all peoples, nations, and languages should serve him; his dominion is an everlasting dominion, which shall not pass away, and his kingdom one that shall not be destroyed. (Daniel 7:13-14)

The Hebrew phrase *son of man* could refer to a human being generically or to a specific individual.[3] When describing his vision, Daniel described a particular person who would be given all authority on earth and reign forever.

Two images stood out in Daniel's mind of the kingdom God would establish when the future iron kingdom began to break apart: 1) a heavenly son of man to rule as King of the world and 2) a rock from heaven that pictured his kingdom growing over all the earth. Daniel wrote down those visions to be remembered when they were fulfilled.[4] He could only wonder what the reality would look like when that Son of Man arrived and his kingdom, like that rock, began to grow.[5]

---

[3] Compare Psalm 8:3-6 with Ezekiel 2:3,6,8.

[4] Daniel 8:26.

[5] If you'd like to follow up on Daniel's remarkable life and visions, I recommend another of my books, *Larger Faith, the Book of Daniel*, Glenn Parkinson, Kindle Direct Publishing, 2020.

§

32 AD

Jesus was born in the days of Caesar Augustus, the first undisputed leader of Rome since it broke into pieces at the death of Julius Caesar. Augustus marked the end of the Roman Republic and the beginning of an Empire that would deteriorate over the next several centuries. Magi from Persia, Babylon's successor, used Daniel's preserved writings to interpret a heavenly sign and arrive to worship the infant Jesus, becoming the first Gentiles to greet the divine King of the whole world.

A man named Simon was also born about the same time. We know nothing of the circumstances except references to his father's name, Jonah or John. Simon's birth had no heavenly fanfare and no wise visitors. Jesus emptied himself to take human form, but Simon inherited a humble station naturally. Jesus' future had been planned from eternity to bring all things in heaven and on earth together in union under God. Simon's life was also pre-planned; like every Jewish boy, he would inherit his father's trade, a fishing business.

Years later, Simon became a disciple of Jesus, who captured the fisherman's heart and imagination. From teaching to healing to miracles, Simon watched Jesus fulfill Old Testament images of the promised Messiah. But for a time, Jesus seemed hesitant to connect the dots about his identity and mission. Everyone knew of Daniel's prophecy, but Jesus would not confirm whether or how it related to him. It was like he was waiting for something.

Then one day, Jesus took his disciples on a spiritual retreat and finally saw what he was waiting for.

> Now when Jesus came into the district of Caesarea Philippi, he asked his disciples, "Who do people say that the Son of Man is?" And they said, "Some say John the Baptist, others say Elijah, and others Jeremiah or one of the prophets." He said to them, "But who do you say that I am?" Simon Peter

replied, "You are the Christ, the Son of the living God." And Jesus answered him, "Blessed are you, Simon Bar-Jonah! For flesh and blood has not revealed this to you, but my Father who is in heaven. And I tell you, you are Peter, and on this rock I will build my church, and the gates of hell shall not prevail against it." (Matthew 16:13-18)

Jesus knew who he was. He had come from heaven to build a kingdom of people reconciled to God from every nation. To be the kingdom *of God*, however, his Heavenly Father had to empower it. For years, Jesus had waited for that power to be exercised.

And then it happened. Simon recognized who Jesus was. The Heavenly Father revealed to this simple fisherman that Jesus was the Son of Man in Daniel's vision. Jesus instantly recognized that God's kingdom—the rock from heaven that Daniel saw—had begun to grow, and not even the powers of hell could stop it now. Simon's nickname, *Rock*, would become the name he would be known by—translated as *Peter* in Greek.

One day, God will institute his kingdom by forcibly re-ordering the whole world according to his original design.[6] But God began that transformation in millions through willing faith in Christ. Peter was the first.[7] Everyone after Peter joins him as part of Daniel's growing and unstoppable rock.

§

If Christians wish to understand discipleship, we should focus on the first Christian disciple. We do that whenever we read one of the Gospels or consider Peter's early leadership in the Church. But Peter also gave us something else. Toward the end of his life, Peter condensed his experience into a concise guide for all who wish to follow Jesus after him. For reasons that will become clear as we go along, I call this guide *Peter's Principles*.

---

[6] John 5:25:29; Philippels 2:9-11; 2 Peter 3:1-9.

[7] Andrew was the first to meet Jesus (John 1:35-40), but Peter was the first to receive divine insight into who Jesus was.

His divine power has granted to us all things that pertain to life and godliness, through the knowledge of him who called us to his own glory and excellence, by which he has granted to us his precious and very great promises, so that through them you may become partakers of the divine nature, having escaped from the corruption that is in the world because of sinful desire.

For this very reason, make every effort to supplement your faith with virtue, and virtue with knowledge, and knowledge with self-control, and self-control with steadfastness, and steadfastness with godliness, and godliness with brotherly affection, and brotherly affection with love.

For if these qualities are yours and are increasing, they keep you from being ineffective or unfruitful in the knowledge of our Lord Jesus Christ. (2 Peter 1:3-8)

Discussion Questions for Chapter 1

1. How would you feel if you discovered that your true birth name was different than the one you grew up with?
2. With Daniel as the background, what did Jesus mean when he called himself "the Son of Man"?
3. Why did Jesus identify Peter as Daniel's rock?
4. How might Peter's experience with Jesus teach us about discipleship?

Chapter 2: The Goal of Discipleship

His divine power has granted to us all things that pertain to life and godliness, through the knowledge of him who called us to his own glory and excellence, by which he has granted to us his precious and very great promises, so that through them you may become partakers of the divine nature, having escaped from the corruption that is in the world because of sinful desire. (2 Peter 1:3-4)

In over 40 years of preaching, I discovered that the most challenging part of crafting a good sermon is knowing what you want to talk about. I can produce pages of thoughts on a Bible passage, with lots of research, sprinkled with clever observations and memorable stories, and still not know precisely what I'm trying to say. There is a big difference between rambling on about many good things and pursuing something truly insightful about one thing. I learned early on that if I'm not sure what I'm talking about, my hearers won't be, either.

I have often recognized that fact when talking to people excited about discipleship. There is usually some training program involved with good things to do but less clarity about the goal. Is discipleship another name for evangelism? Is it a tactic for personal growth, church growth, or social change? Is the primary goal that disciples replicate themselves? If so, what exactly do they hope to replicate? How do you measure discipleship? How do you know if it is successful or effective? Does all religious activity count as discipleship? Is it a program? Can it be programmed? To answer such questions, we must start with a clear sense of what discipleship is meant to accomplish.

The original meaning of discipleship was an apprenticeship: basic training for a craft that prepares the apprentice to practice that craft for a lifetime. My first year of college in 1969 included an apprenticeship in computer programming that taught me a simple programming language. Although the language wasn't used for high-end projects, it embodied the fundamental concepts of declaring variables, loops, subroutines, branching, input, output, etc. I discovered that having learned the basics with a simple language, I could quickly go on to learn other more useful computer languages available at the time, such as Assembly, Basic, Fortran, or C. The syntax differed in each case, but the basic concepts were the same. My initial apprenticeship in the basics of programming enabled me to go as far with that craft as I wished. Similarly, I learned construction techniques in my High School shop class by building simple assignments. I have used those same techniques ever since for various real-world projects.

If disciples are people who follow Christ, discipleship must be an initial apprenticeship that teaches us how to do so. It is training in how to be involved as the risen Jesus builds the kingdom of God within us and throughout the earth.[1]

The kingdom of God

The Apostle Peter describes the restoration of God's rule or kingdom in verses 3-4, and what he says is astonishing. Our calling in Christ is to "become partakers of the divine nature." No matter how often I read that, it always causes me to pause. I don't think many Christians would describe discipleship as preparing us for this. Training to become like God! Is that possible? Is that even a good thing? After all, Satan tempted

---

[1] Mark 1:15-16; Acts 1:6-8; 1 Corinthians 15:20-28.

Eve by telling her that eating the forbidden fruit would make her like God. Yet, that's what Peter said, so we should grasp his meaning before we start and be sure we want to spend our lives journeying toward this destination.

Another way that Peter expresses our calling is "life and godliness." This clarifies that Peter is not implying that we can become divine but is talking about how we can reflect God's nature in our humanity. Peter's words echo God's command in Genesis for us to display his image and likeness through our dominion over the earth, something called *the Cultural Mandate*:

> Then God said, "Let us make man in our image, after our likeness. And let them have dominion over the fish of the sea and over the birds of the heavens and over the livestock and over all the earth and over every creeping thing that creeps on the earth."
>
> So God created man in his own image, in the image of God he created him; male and female he created them.
>
> And God blessed them. And God said to them, "Be fruitful and multiply and fill the earth and subdue it, and have dominion over the fish of the sea and over the birds of the heavens and over every living thing that moves on the earth." (Genesis 1:26-28)

Mankind was created to represent God on the earth by causing it to flourish. To use a modern word, God created mankind to develop a *civilization* that develops the world to its full potential in terms of usefulness and beauty.[2] Such a civilization requires many human beings, which implies a society that works together to exercise dominion over the planet in a way that manifests God's goodness.

Since the early church fathers, Christians have wondered if there is a difference between the *image* of God and the *likeness* of God. Fortunately, most views tend to cover similar ground. I believe that image refers to mankind's position in creation,

---

[2] Note how God's design for Eden is described in those terms in Genesis 1:8-9.

while likeness refers to our ability to act in that position as God would. Think of the difference between the office of President and how well a specific person carries out that office.

Let me now exchange civilization for the equivalent Old Testament term, *kingdom*. God created mankind to build a kingdom. This is phrased as a command, so we can say that God created mankind with the mission to build his kingdom on earth. God rules everywhere, of course. The kingdom of God on earth is the perfect civilization we are charged to create on this planet. We are in God's *image* because he gave us the mission of imitating his rule of all things on earth.

Likeness refers to the human capacity to carry out our mission. Intellectual intelligence, emotional intelligence, organizational skills, and many mental and physical abilities contribute to that capacity. The crucial component is moral character, ruling ourselves and the planet according to God's goodness.

Humanity's violent, wasteful, and tragic tale began when our first parents used their freedom to choose whether or not to respect God's definition of right and wrong.[3] Their refusal to do so morally twisted them and their children. As a result, the patches of civilization we create—from families to businesses to nations—are not the models of God's goodness we were created to build.[4]

When God spoke of humanity's likeness to himself, he also characterized it as a marriage that generates children.[5] This implies structured and loving relationships in which humanity works together as an extended family to model God's rule. Since Adam was considered God's child,[6] we could say that God wanted his kingdom on earth to be a family project. But sadly, choosing the right to define life as we please has not

---

[3] Genesis 2:15-17.
[4] Romans 1:18-25.
[5] Genesis 1:27-28.
[6] Luke 3:38.

reliably produced loving relationships structured as God designed.

Therefore, while it is still our responsibility as God's image to care for the earth, we no longer possess God's moral and relational likeness to do the job as intended. We create a succession of individual lives, families, and cultures, but none adequately reflects God's character or love. None last forever. Like the succession of empires Daniel saw, one replaces another throughout history.

But in Bethlehem, the divine likeness finally appeared to build a kingdom worthy of our Creator. The Son of God is uniquely divine, but in the true form of a human being, he is God's perfect image and likeness. Therefore, partaking of the divine nature means sharing the image and likeness of God that is manifested in Christ's humanity:

> For those whom he foreknew he also predestined to be conformed to the image of his Son, in order that he might be the firstborn among many brothers. (Romans 8:29)

This means that the Cultural Mandate and the Great Commission—to make disciples of every nation—are the same command to build God's kingdom on earth, except that the first was given before human sin and the second after Christ's redemption was accomplished. With all authority in heaven and on earth, Jesus commissioned his Church to teach disciples to obey everything he commanded, which ultimately takes us back to the Cultural Mandate. The difference is that saving faith in Christ is now required to deal with the guilt and power of sin, enabling us to escape "the corruption that is in the world because of sinful desire" so we can begin to be and do what we were initially made for. As God's character and love grow in us, we influence everyone and everything we touch, and the kingdom of God expands until Christ returns to perfect all things.

Finding ourselves in Christ

Through a vision, Daniel understood that the Son of Man's future kingdom would be different than any other. It would involve people from every nation, glorify God, and never end.[7] In essence, the kingdoms of this world change national boundaries and political leadership while leaving people essentially unchanged. The kingdom of the Son of Man does the opposite. It ignores national boundaries and works under any political leadership to change people. Ultimately, Jesus will restore God's rule over this planet in every conceivable sense, but until he completes his Church, Jesus restores the rule of God in individuals. Jesus expands the kingdom of God by transforming those who will follow him from sinners to saints, alienated to reconciled, rebels to loyalists, guilty to forgiven, unclean to holy, orphaned to adopted, barren to beloved, clueless to commissioned, lost to found, and from dying to forever alive. The kingdom of God is about Jesus remaking people into the image and likeness of our Creator.

Discipleship prepares me to live in this kingdom by teaching me that the sense of purpose and identity I've grown up with is not wholly appropriate. The values of success and expectations for relationships that I have adopted are misguided. My conscience is confused. The way I love is flawed. My handling of the planet is chaotic. My sense of responsibility to my fellow man is stunted. I was meant for God's constant fellowship, but his presence is vague at best. All this has shaped how I understand who I am and why I'm alive.

God, however, knows who he designed me to be, and I will fully comprehend that identity in God's completed and everlasting kingdom. This is reflected in a profound vision given to the Apostle John in the Book of Revelation:

> He who has an ear, let him hear what the Spirit says to the churches. To the one who conquers I will give some of the hidden manna, and I will give him a white stone, with *a new*

---

[7] Daniel 7:13-14.

name written on the stone that no one knows except the one who receives it. (Revelation 2:17, *emphasis added*)

The name I received at birth, my "Simon" name if you will, reflects my time and place in history, along with the tastes of my Mom and Dad. In my fallenness, I spend my life using this name as I try to comprehend who I am and why I exist. My sense of self formed from my place in history, social demographic, favorite TV characters, movie plots, parental expectations, native language, national politics, Grandma's tenderness, Uncle Joe's profanity, adolescent sexual confusion, playground victories, taunts of bullies, and whatever I post that's rewarded with likes. These are artifacts of where and how I was born and the small selection of experiences I've had in my short life. They establish my particular heritage of cultural insights and blind spots, opportunities, limitations, perspectives, and prejudices. Eventually, my identity settled down to a few relationships, a career, and a handful of fantasies. This crazy quilt of influences may color in some of God's image and likeness, but the design is neither consistent nor complete. All this is represented by the name my parents gave me.

But my *real* name, like Peter's name, is given only by God because only he appreciates my destined purpose and specific place in his kingdom. In John's vision, Jesus promises I will know my purpose perfectly one day. But from the first day of faith in Jesus, I begin to discover that God's purpose in creating me is not necessarily found in the things I grew up feeling, believing, and doing. Christ will gladly affirm whatever in me already points toward God's design, but he will also faithfully expose in me what Peter called the corruption of the world. I follow Jesus because I'm confident he knows who I am meant to be, even as I still seek to discover it. I am meant to be like him.

Beloved, we are God's children now, and what we will be has not yet appeared; but we know that when he appears we shall be like him, because we shall see him as

he is. And everyone who thus hopes in him purifies himself
as he is pure. (1 John 3:2-2)

Salvation sets me on a journey to replicate Christ's God-
centered human nature. Faith in Christ brings the complete
forgiveness of sin upfront, so the journey is not motivated by
threat but by promise. Perfection will come in fullness at the
renewal of all things. But when Peter says we already have
everything needed for life and godliness, he declares that this
transformation has already begun. Eternal life begins when
my faith in Christ awakens, and the Holy Spirit fashions a new
me with a restored relationship with God.[8]

Therefore, if anyone is in Christ, he is a new creation. The
old has passed away; behold, the new has come.
(2 Corinthians 5:17)

A new believer remains the same person but with the seed of a
new spiritual DNA.[9] Discipleship teaches me how to
progressively discover my new self as I transform into the
spiritual likeness of Jesus.

Gospel faith transforms different people in predictable
ways as they find themselves in the same person: Jesus.
Imagine two non-Christians as different from each other as
possible. One works for a big government agency, and the
other is a domestic terrorist. They are different people, with
different agendas, from different demographics,
fundamentally at odds politically, economically, socially, and
perhaps even violently. Their dreams for themselves and the
nation could not be further apart. But now imagine that
somehow, they each become solidly converted to follow Jesus
as Christian disciples. And imagine that they even find
themselves in the same fellowship. What would happen?

At first, perhaps each would be confident that Christ
would turn the other to his way of thinking. But as they are

---

[8] John 17:3.
[9] Titus 3:3-8; 1 John 3:9.

discipled, something else happens. They each discover that some of their previous worldviews reflected divine wisdom, and some did not. Their gaze shifts from the real speck in the other man's eye to the log in their own. Their repentance counters the specific sins which their backgrounds and choices had shaped. Having received forgiveness from God, they each forgive the other for offenses arising from their past lives. Ultimately, they would learn to love each other more than they had ever selflessly loved anyone. The best of their former selves would be pruned, grafted, and integrated with new Jesus-shaped elements to build lives, families, churches, and a world that reflect God's goodness. This process happens to everyone who is discipled by Jesus.

Peter knew this was true because he saw the above example with his own eyes. He saw Matthew, the tax collector for Rome, become the brother of Simon (not Peter), the Zealot who fomented violent revolution against Rome. Peter saw both of them leave the sins of their past nailed to Jesus' cross and then rise with Christ into the kingdom of God. Peter watched them become disciples of the Master and then become brothers. It wasn't that they came to appreciate each other's point of view. Instead, they both adopted Jesus' point of view, which is to say that they embraced the path of his character and love as the one they wished to travel. Through gospel witness that reflected their distinct interests and strengths, that same transformation spread to very different cultures.[10]

At some point, Peter realized that what he saw in the other disciples was happening in him, too. The Gospels and Acts record his transformation, and 2 Peter 1:3-8 summarizes how it happened.

Never has such transformation been more urgent. America is losing sight of any true meaning to life, so people celebrate their limited experiences and chaotic feelings as their authentic selves. The new self I discover in Christ is so much more. God

---

[10] Matthew is credited with ministry in Ethiopia and Simon the (former) Zealot in Persia.

re-created me to live like Jesus, love like Jesus, and accomplish many things Jesus accomplished.[11]

Apart from Christ, my life is like one of those sticky roller things used to pick up cat hair from clothes and furniture, random lint that's adhered to my soul over the years. I look at all the bits and pieces and try hard to find a pattern, but there is none.

Then I discover that Jesus is my pattern. Individual aspects of my body, skills, talents, and personality are my own, for the Lord loves variety. But my intended character and capacity to love are fully present in Jesus Christ, and I have been predestined to be conformed to it. As that occurs, God's kingdom rule is extended within me. As his rule expands in me, it shapes my relationships. Finally, as my relationships are reshaped, they frame my place in Christ's mission.

Discipleship and mission

The Church's mission is to make disciples. But disciples are more than people who are saved at a point in time. Disciples are people in whom the kingdom of God is growing and who are becoming kingdom-makers. They glorify God by being the image and likeness of God in every area of life.

At its core, the mission of the Church is more organic than organizational. Disciples cannot be effectively recruited into Christ's mission by outside influences. Rather, it is when we find our new identity in Jesus that his love compels us from the inside to join him in extending the kingdom of God.[12] And it is the reality and witness of Christ's life within us that the Holy Spirit uses to stimulate gospel faith in others.[13]

§

The goal of discipleship is not for me to get saved because salvation marks the beginning and not the end of my journey.

---

[11] John 14:12.
[12] 2 Corinthians 5:14-15.
[13] 1 Thessalonians 1:4-10.

The goal of discipleship is not to use Jesus to help me attain whatever dreams I bring to him. The goal of discipleship is not to gain some doctrine, become familiar with spiritual disciplines like prayer and evangelism, or join a church, although all those things are involved.

The goal of discipleship is to learn how to follow Jesus so I can discover in him who I am. This is how the kingdom of God will expand in me and eventually through me.

I want this. I want following Jesus to be why I get up in the morning. Come to think of it, for three years, following Jesus was literally why Peter got up in the morning. And when Jesus left to direct the Church from Heaven, Peter kept getting up each day for the same reason. That's what I want, too.

So how do I follow Jesus to discover the new me that he is forming? The first Christian disciple answers that question with seven ordered steps.

Discussion Questions for Chapter 2

1. Use items you are carrying to introduce yourself.
    a) Do you think your introduction encompasses everything that God designed you to be?
2. Review Peter's thoughts through 2 Peter 1:3-4 by answering each question directly from the associated quote.
    a) *His divine power has granted to us all things that pertain to life and godliness,*
       How does God manifest his power in our lives?
    b) *through the knowledge of him [Christ] who called us to his own glory and excellence,*
       How does God convey his power to us?
    c) *by which he has granted to us his precious and very great promises,*
       How do we activate God's power in us?
    d) *so that through them you may become partakers of the divine nature, having escaped from the corruption that is in the world because of sinful desire.*
       What does God's power in us accomplish?
3. How are the Great Commission and Cultural Mandate related?
    a) What does the Great Commission add to the Cultural Mandate?

Chapter 3: The Steps of Discipleship

For this very reason, make every effort to supplement your faith with virtue, and virtue with knowledge, and knowledge with self-control, and self-control with steadfastness, and steadfastness with godliness, and godliness with brotherly affection, and brotherly affection with love. (2 Peter 1:5-7)

I have come back to this passage often for over 30 years. In between, I practiced discipleship by pursuing a variety of spiritual disciplines. Like many Christians, I've used prayer, Bible memorization, small groups, evangelism, and personal retreats. I've tasted different worship styles, planted churches in neighboring communities, and supported missions overseas. I've fasted for as long as five days, prayed face down on the floor, let my praise resonate in nature, spent long stretches in silent listening, and sampled the biographies of noteworthy and memorable Christians. I've used or studied various discipleship programs: some stress personal holiness, some worship, and some evangelism and multiplication. In my pastoral ministry, I have chosen bits and pieces of them all. It has been a rewarding ride but not a focused one. And always, I've come back to 2 Peter 1:5-7.

"For this reason" connects a list of seven qualities with what Peter wrote in verses 3-4 about God's power to overcome the damage of sin and enable me to become the human being

God intended me to be. Looking ahead to verse 8, he will make the audacious claim that cultivating these qualities never fails—*never* fails—to manifest God's transforming power. My approach to discipleship has been unorganized and piecemeal, with sporadic results. Yet Peter described something surprisingly specific and guaranteed to bring the kingdom of God into my life and through me to others.

What could be so special about this sequential list of qualities? The Bible mentions many good qualities. Why is brotherly affection included and peace or hope not? The Apostle Paul made lists of sins, virtues, and spiritual gifts which are neither complete nor sequential. Consider this example from Paul:

> But the fruit of the Spirit is love, joy, peace, patience, kindness, goodness, faithfulness, gentleness, self-control. (Galatians 5:22-23)

This is a simple, partial, and unordered list. Items are mentioned one after another, but there is no reason to think that Paul considered the order significant. He could have listed kindness first and patience last, and it would make no difference whatsoever.

Peter's list, however, is an explicit sequence. That's indicated by the word *supplement*. The word means adding something else to something already there—not more of the same thing—but adding a new thing. Seven qualities are to be supplemented to faith in a carefully specific order. Why is this list of qualities, in this order, so significant?

One reason for my early attraction to physics was watching relationships and patterns emerge from data analysis. When I became a Christian in college, I was happy to discover that Bible study shared that commonality with physics. Observed data (the Bible text) must be repeatedly analyzed until the pattern of God's mind emerges. So I was determined to keep returning to Peter's text until I understood the significance of its pattern.

In 1971, when my college fellowship taught me how to study the Bible, they gave me a memorable true story of a beloved teacher often used as a parable about observation, *The Student, the Fish, and Agassiz.* I have included it as an Appendix and encourage you to enjoy it. A student is tasked to examine a preserved fish without instrumentation but using only his senses. It takes him three days to notice what the professor considers the most critical, prominent, and conspicuous coordinating feature. What does the good professor teach through this? "Facts are stupid things," he would say, "until brought into connection with some general law."

Compared to me, that student was a genius. I looked at Peter's text for decades before I finally appreciated the pattern, Peter's organizing idea. As it was with the fish, it is entirely self-evident. I had seen it, you see it, and when I mention it, you may wonder why it's a big deal. It's a big deal because it turns a simple list into an actionable process for change that I'm sure Peter used to disciple thousands and that I can use today. Please allow me to point out the obvious. We begin with verse 5:

> For this very reason, make every effort to supplement your faith with virtue.

Since Peter addresses Christians, Peter treats faith as a given. That is why it is not added to anything. Faith must already be present before discipleship can proceed further. Peter then instructs us to make an effort to add virtue to our faith. We will spend an entire chapter on each of these qualities, but for now, let me characterize virtue as a desire for goodness. To become like Jesus, we must make an effort to add to our faith the desire to be like him.

Notice the immense importance of the order. We are not saved by first expending great effort to seek goodness and eventually being saved. Salvation doesn't work that way. We are saved by simple faith in gospel grace. There is no effort on our part; salvation is accomplished entirely by Jesus' effort. Having been saved, we must then supplement our faith if we want to be transformed by the most wonderful person who ever lived. To become like Jesus, the first step after faith is to apply honest, consistent effort to cultivate the desire to find ourselves in him. The point is that virtue rests on faith and not the other way around. The power of this list comes not only from what items are in it but also from the order that the qualities support one another.

At this point, if Peter went on to list all seven steps from faith to love, they would all rest on gospel faith. But he does not do that. Instead, he continues:

> For this very reason, make every effort to supplement your faith with virtue, and virtue with knowledge ...

Unlike a simple list, virtue is repeated and explicitly given a different function. First, it is something added, and then it is something to which you add something else. In other words, virtue is added to saving faith, but knowledge is not added to saving faith; it is added to virtue. Peter is inescapably specific about this. Hmmm. That makes sense, though. If you desire to be good like Jesus, you need to understand what that means; you need knowledge. Knowledge would be wasted, however, if added to saving faith *without also having the desire to use it*. This ordering may seem trivially obvious, but it has enormous practical applications. Knowledge is most useful when eagerly consumed by the desire for virtue and not when force-fed directly to saving faith.

Peter repeats this pattern with all seven qualities until he gets to love. Each quality is the next logical step toward love. Each grows best out of the one just before it and is the best soil to produce the one just after it. In the larger picture, each step needs the support of everything before and is necessary to support everything after. Finally, the list ends with love. Love is the ultimate fruit of God's kingdom within me and is the crucial quality that bears kingdom fruit in others (see the diagram).

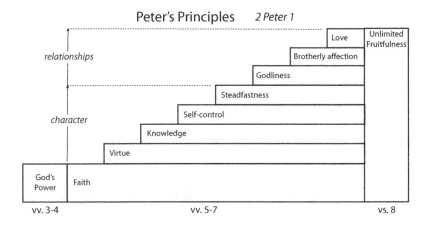

Peter's Principles   *2 Peter 1*

| | | Love | Unlimited Fruitfulness |
| Brotherly affection |
| Godliness |
| Steadfastness |
| Self-control |
| Knowledge |
| Virtue |
| God's Power | Faith |

relationships

character

vv. 3-4   vv. 5-7   vs. 8

The more you ponder this pattern, the more practical it appears. As in a staircase, if a step is missing, it becomes difficult to climb further. If two steps in a row are missing, it becomes very difficult indeed. Peter's structured list makes it clear that stepping directly from faith to Christ-like love and effective ministry is virtually impossible. Christ-like love is a learned quality, and it is learned in steps. Having established that God's power to transform us is administered through promises, Peter lists these steps as the way to apply God's promises. This is how the Holy Spirit wishes to work with us.

Wow. Suddenly a random-looking list is electric with internal dynamics. Emotions, knowledge, action, and relationships are related in specific ways, some of which may be surprising. For example, in the chapters ahead, we will explore how the earlier steps, which relate to character, support the later steps that develop relationships. In other words, Christ-like relationships are supported by Christ-like character and not simply by our feelings. That sounds important. We will see equally significant implications in how each step relates to those above and below.

This is like learning the secret recipe for Coca-Cola: start with this, add this, then this, do this and this, and you get something out of this world (a tribute to my wife, a true Coke fan). If you have the recipe, anyone could make this stuff! When it comes to discipleship, Peter gives us a recipe.

§

The rest of this book will examine Peter's list in detail, so it might be wise to deal first with reasonable concerns about this take on it. I believe these concerns are reasonable because I've had to work through them myself.

Why are these particular qualities so special?

For some time, I wondered why these qualities were highlighted because they hardly represent all the qualities of Christ-likeness. What about hope or joy? What about patience or kindness? What about justice or mercy?

I was stumped until I realized how discipleship is distinct from spiritual growth in general. Spiritual growth is broad and life-long, involving every aspect of God's likeness in Christ. But since discipleship is a kind of apprenticeship, it only trains me in *how to grow* in any area. It focuses on the seven ordered qualities that build character and love, thus preparing a believer for kingdom growth in a hundred contexts. Whether the area of spiritual growth is marriage and the family, personal worship, evangelism, bringing wisdom to public policy, or anything else, the growth steps are always the same. In every case, the goal is *always* to develop Christ-like character and love.

In other words, Peter's seven steps don't teach me everything Jesus commands; they teach me how to be a good student. Think of it this way. There are a gazillion different crafts one could master, from baking to statecraft to archery to sculpting to landscaping and many more. They are all different. But learning any of them requires similar elements: opportunity, interest, study, demonstration of basic skills, practice until competence is achieved, trust in the instructor, working well with fellow students, and finally, going off on your own into the wide world to practice what you learned.

I just paraphrased Peter's list. They are the qualities of a student, applied to character and love instead of archery or baking. Discipleship doesn't train us in everything Christ commanded. It trains us how to pursue everything he commanded. Maturity as a *disciple* is the work of a lifetime. To be *discipled* is to be initially prepared to be a faithful and competent follower of Jesus.

Why is the careful structure of this list so essential for spiritual growth?

Peter doesn't give a simple, unordered list of qualities. Instead, he takes care to structure them in an intentional sequence. The reason for that becomes increasingly apparent as we study them in detail, and the logic becomes clear. The need for a sequence isn't surprising, though. It's similar to introductory training in any endeavor. There are best practices and a logical way to do things.

Serving behind an ice cream counter in Cambridge, Massachusetts, certainly wasn't rocket science. Even so, I needed an hour's apprenticeship to be brought up to speed on how to use the cash register, change ice cream drums, properly scoop the ice cream to leave nothing in the drums, anticipate the need for resupply, handle the trash, and learn company policy. (For example, I could eat as much ice cream for free as I wanted. I did. Got sick. Never thought I would eat ice cream again. Lesson learned.) The job required initial training, so I could do the work the way the owner knew was most efficient. I had to learn what he wanted to be done at the beginning of my shift so that I could serve customers efficiently and then prepare everything for the next shift. Only after some experience could I see why things were taught as he instructed me. I had different but similar training for working as a computer operator for the State of Maryland, a security guard for a defense contractor, a hospital janitor, and a pastoral intern. I imagine you had similar initial training in your various jobs.

Doing almost anything new begins with learning how it is done. Some people can teach themselves how to play the electric organ (my Dad did), but most people need lessons (truthfully, my Dad could have used lessons). Music teachers approach training in a specific order of steps so students can always learn the next thing by building on what they already know. A good tennis instructor will not allow students to solidify bad habits by playing tennis for months before teaching them how to correctly hold and swing the racket. That should be taught upfront so students learn how to play effectively. Only then will advanced points of tennis strategy be accessible.

Similarly, Christians should become familiar with the process of how character and love are formed because that is what the Holy Spirit will be doing with them for the rest of their lives to prepare them to join Jesus in his mission. We become like Christ by the power of God, and there is a specific order to how we access this power from faith to love. This means that there are simple but specific dynamics to spiritual growth that disciples should be taught:

Spiritual power requires each quality in Peter's list to connect with the ones before and after. Think of a car's drive train, the transmission, differential, driveshaft, axles, CV joints, and wheels. Motive power goes in one direction. Each component must be installed in the correct relationship to the one before it and the one after. The same components assembled in the wrong order won't work. Each part will pass along power only if all the pieces in front of it are passing power down. If a part breaks or operates inefficiently, power is compromised everywhere down the line. Similarly, each of Peter's elements must be included. None can be skipped, and they must operate in the correct order.

Spiritual power requires all seven component elements to operate simultaneously, like a garden hose. Faith is the spigot; it must be turned on. Love is the life-giving water spraying from the nozzle everywhere it points. In between, the hose must be unobstructed throughout. Wherever there is a kink or clog, the flow will be restricted downstream from that point. This is similar to the first dynamic mentioned but stresses that qualities may not be retired after they are first attained. Every quality must continuously operate to produce love.

Spiritual power is exercised when we move from one step to the next. Continued spiritual growth requires change and development. Change happens when we make a move from one of Peter's steps to the next, such as using biblical knowledge to craft new obedience or letting my love for God overflow in expanded love for God's people. Peter is not suggesting that we fully develop a single aspect of Christ-likeness from faith to love and then start on another. Christians typically face growth challenges and opportunities in several areas at once. In each area of spiritual growth, we stand on one of Peter's steps. We experience God's power when we move on to whichever step is next.

Apprenticeship is about learning how a craft works and how to practice it. When learning soccer, conducting an archeological dig, mastering a second language, playing the oboe, or grilling a steak, it is important to understand the natural flow involved. If we don't, we will work against ourselves, sabotaging our efforts by forgetting steps, trying to force results the wrong way, and expecting an outcome before it can possibly happen. There is a particular order, a specific flow to God's power to transform us. Once disciples learn this, they are prepared for a lifetime of spiritual growth.

Isn't it simplistic to reduce discipleship to a recipe?

It feels like spiritual growth is being reduced to a bread machine—push these buttons, in this order, and out pops a delicious Christian. I was helped here by a comment attributed to Ted Williams, one of the most successful batters in baseball history. Someone once belittled his achievements: "After all, hitting a ball with a bat is pretty simple stuff." "You're right," Williams replied. "It is simple, but it's not easy."

Peter's list seems remarkably straightforward once you become familiar with it, but Peter says it will require *every effort.* This is the process Jesus taught Peter that the Holy Spirit uses to transform people twisted by sin into the persons God meant for us to be. It truly is simple, but it's not easy.

Aren't spiritual disciplines like Bible study and prayer enough for spiritual growth?

No, not if I pursue them as ends in themselves. They are necessary to exercise the qualities Peter mentions, but they will not connect those qualities automatically. If I practice spiritual disciplines religiously without consciously trying to cultivate Christ-like character (obedience) and relationships (love), then I am not using those disciplines effectively. In that case, I'm corralling spiritual power that I never harness to do work.

God's kingdom is built with Jesus' character and love, not with prayers or Bible studies that do not seek those things. Spiritual disciplines become indispensable for the kingdom only when they are used to travel Peter's steps toward Christ-likeness.

Doesn't managing a process discourage reliance on the Holy Spirit?

I came to see that when I asked this, I was confusing the spiritual with the magical. Being made right with God (justification) is entirely the work of Christ. Spiritual growth (sanctification) is not. That involves both God and me. The Holy Spirit has not been sent to magically make me grow while I remain passive. He has been sent to travel alongside me and be my Helper as I make an epic journey. I cannot follow Christ without the Holy Spirit, but he will not follow Christ for me. He provides the promised power for transformation, but he is not the one who needs to change.

In the next chapter, Peter refers to what Christ called "bearing fruit." This is related to God's purpose in sending his Spirit to manifest Jesus in the world.[1] The Holy Spirit helps us find ourselves in Jesus and responds to our growing Christ-

---

[1] John 15:26, 16:14-15; 1 Corinthians 12:3.

likeness by expanding God's kingdom in and through us in ways we could never achieve by ourselves.

§

Salvation is about simple faith in Jesus' work for me. In theory, I could genuinely trust in Jesus, never do a day's work to become like him, and still be saved. But in reality, no Christian wants to do that. A reborn heart yearns to walk with Jesus. Discipleship is learning how to discover my redeemed identity. I don't want to wait until I'm buried before I find out who I am.

When I've learned how to practice these qualities as Peter presents them, I'm ready to spend the rest of my life working with the Holy Spirit to become like Jesus in dozens of ways. I will have been discipled like Peter was. What I do with that training is up to me.

Our overview of Peter's text brings us to the last section and a staggering promise.

Discussion Questions for Chapter 3

1. Share an experience (good or bad) of putting something together. For example, a piece of furniture or a toy, a wedding or party, choosing a college or a new house—anything that required a number of steps.
   a) How did it go?
   b) Can you think of two steps in the process that had a logical relationship—one had to be done before the other?
2. What study skills would a college student need regardless of their major?
   a) Apply this notion to discipleship.
3. Do you think every Christian would benefit from a practical introduction to following Jesus?
   a) What was the best part of your introduction?
   b) Could you have used more training?
4. The chapter includes a list of reasonable concerns about this way of understanding discipleship.
   a) Do you think they were addressed adequately?

Chapter 4: Effective Discipleship

For if these qualities are yours and are increasing, they keep you from being ineffective or unfruitful in the knowledge of our Lord Jesus Christ. (2 Peter 1:8)

One way to assess a product is to look at the manufacturer's warranty. How confident are the people who made this thing that it will work reliably? In the case of Peter's list, the manufacturer is the Holy Spirit. His warranty is unique, for it absolutely guarantees that if we apply these qualities as directed, God's kingdom will grow. No exceptions.

A journey that takes me somewhere

Peter says that the process he outlines is guaranteed to avoid ineffectiveness. The implication is that discipleship efforts could be ineffective. It's possible to go through discipleship programs without personal transformation in moral character or love, thus gaining little we can contribute to Christ's mission. We tend not to notice such failure when our eyes are not on the right goal. It's common to think of discipleship in terms of activity (its technique) rather than Christ-likeness (its goal), so we feel successful just by finishing a program or learning new spiritual ideas and ministry skills.

Discipleship is initial training in how to find myself in Jesus. It is only effective training when I actually become a little more like him. This requires some change in the way I see

God, myself, and the world—an inner change that naturally results in new outward actions. An apprenticeship is ineffective if the graduate still can't do what is needed for the job. Therefore, my discipleship is unsuccessful when I only learn about godly choices or the meaning of love. It becomes successful when I actually make a godly choice and treat somebody more lovingly. I think of a line from a *Peanuts* cartoon strip: "I love mankind … it's people I can't stand!"[1] That describes the problem with what is sometimes considered "success" in discipleship: learning how we *ought* to live without any practical change.

Since it is only initial training, changes during discipleship may be small; they need only demonstrate that I know how to apply Peter's process. The point is to learn by experience that transformation in me is possible and worth the effort. While my spiritual growth is never complete in this life, discipleship should enable me to begin exchanging a lifestyle that was sewn from the world's fashions for one tailored according to Jesus' design.

While transformation does not always happen overnight or at a fast pace, it sometimes does happen overnight and always at some pace once I understand how God's power and promises work. Appreciating the long-term transformation of who I am may only come later upon reflection. Peter's story in the Gospels, Acts, and Epistles is a later reflection on the life-long trek from Simon, the fisherman, to Peter the Apostle. From his first encounter with Christ, the New Testament traces how Simon changed, his lifestyle changed, his decisions changed, and his attitudes and prejudices changed. This was not so I could marvel at how Simon found his true identity in Jesus, but rather so I could anticipate doing the same.

Every Christian stands at the beginning of such a journey when they come to faith. Discipleship teaches how to work with Christ's Spirit as he enfolds my life into God's kingdom. It is basic training for following Jesus. The process is not

---

[1] This line was spoken by Linus Van Pelt in the November 12, 1959 comic strip of *Peanuts*, written and drawn by Charles Schulz

complicated, but it is specific and must be learned to be effective. Spiritual growth is meant to be a journey. Discipleship trains us how to travel so that the trip actually takes us somewhere.

The trellis for a fruitful vine

In verse 8, Peter links effectiveness with fruitfulness. They go together. Effectiveness has to do with the personal transformation that discipleship enables. Fruitfulness has to do with the result of that transformation. That is to say, when discipleship is effective, it is naturally fruitful.

> I am the true vine, and my Father is the vinedresser. Every branch in me that does not bear fruit he takes away, and every branch that does bear fruit he prunes, that it may bear more fruit. Already you are clean because of the word that I have spoken to you. Abide in me, and I in you. As the branch cannot bear fruit by itself, unless it abides in the vine, neither can you, unless you abide in me. I am the vine; you are the branches ...
>
> By this my Father is glorified, that you bear much fruit and so prove to be my disciples. (John 15:1-8)

Fruit refers to a dual manifestation of God's kingdom. The fruit of the Spirit naturally grows *within me* as my character more resembles Jesus.[2] Fruit also refers to God's kingdom expanding *through me* as my words and life point others to Christ.[3] Fruit is a biblical metaphor for both my own spiritual growth and my impact on Christ's kingdom. When you read "fruit," think of sanctification and ministry.

Effective discipleship indirectly causes fruitfulness. Why indirectly? Because discipleship's goal is to replicate Jesus' character and love. As those things develop, they produce fruit *automatically*—not that fruit requires no effort, but because effective sanctification and ministry are the natural products of

---

[2] Galatians 5:16-24.
[3] John 4:34-41.

Christ's character and love. Think of it this way. A vine's branches do not try to be fruitful. They simply *are* productive when they are healthy and well-tended. That is their nature. It takes work to support a vine's productivity, but when it has support, it bears fruit all by itself naturally. My Heavenly Father, the vinedresser, trains me to tend the vineyard with him, building a trellis that exposes the branches to sunshine, water, and nourishment. The fruitfulness of God's kingdom is not the immediate goal or focus of discipleship training. Instead, it becomes the inevitable result of the trellis that discipleship teaches us to build.

If my apprenticeship in following Jesus were to focus immediately on my behavior or ministry, it would ignore the vinedresser's training and uselessly expect my branches to produce as they lie tangled on the ground. I might be tempted to preach to them, argue with them, bribe them, or pray over them for magical results, but none of that is what the vinedresser says my branches need to draw life from the vine. Instead, I must direct my prayers and action to construct a trellis of virtue, knowledge, self-control, steadfastness, godliness, brotherly affection, and love. This is the sunshine, water, and nutrients that my branches need to grow fruit on their own. Look at how Jesus described it:

> The kingdom of God is as if a man should scatter seed on the ground. He sleeps and rises night and day, and *the seed sprouts and grows; he knows not how. The earth produces by itself*, first the blade, then the ear, then the full grain in the ear. But when the grain is ripe, at once he puts in the sickle, because the harvest has come. (Mark 4:26-29, *emphasis added*)

Like a farmer, we are responsible for working hard to establish the right conditions for growth. When we do, growth happens; we "know not how" because that is what adequately supported plants naturally do. This applies both to kingdom fruitfulness in me and through me. In me, the kingdom manifests itself as who I am, the aroma of Christ. The kingdom manifests itself through me as that aroma attracts or repels others.[4] Attempting to artificially replicate a scent that's naturally generated by character and love won't succeed and is entirely unnecessary.[5]

Peter describes how the Holy Spirit works differently than we often suppose. Typically, our focus in discipleship is laboring for kingdom expansion, assuming that character and love will take care of themselves. Peter says that this is backward. Instead, he tells us to prioritize developing Christ's character and love. As we do, the Holy Spirit causes God's kingdom to expand naturally—in fact, you couldn't stop it if you tried. This distinction is worth pondering because it is crucial to understanding how discipleship works.

Another important insight is that if I perceive a lack of fruitfulness, I know that the problem lies with at least one transfer point between Peter's seven qualities. By describing the process the Holy Spirit uses to apply the power of God, Peter gives us a powerful diagnostic tool to identify the underlying cause of any spiritual stagnation.

The logic is powerful: Christ said that we bear fruit *only* as we abide in him. Peter states that applying these seven ordered steps *always* results in fruit. Therefore, with these steps, Peter explains how to abide in Christ.

The Peter Principle or Peter's Principles?

"Every employee tends to rise to his level of incompetence."[6] This maxim from Lawrence J. Peter has been successfully applied to various infrastructures, from education to politics to the military. People tend to be promoted when they do their job well and stop being promoted when they no longer excel. This often happens when a successful employee is rewarded with an administrative position requiring very

---

[4] 2 Corinthians 2:15-16.

[5] Note how Paul follows up the last referenced Scripture with 2 Corinthians 2:17.

[6] *The Peter Principle*, Laurence J. Peter and Raymond Hull, Harper Collins, 2009, Kindle location 446.

different skills than the ones that earlier made them successful. One could humorously speculate that all those in the highest leadership positions are incompetent. Or, more realistically, what makes you succeed at the beginning may not bring success at higher levels. In a career, people typically rise until they reach a plateau where they cannot go any higher. This is known as *The Peter Principle*.

The Peter Principle reminds me of a parallel reality that many Christians experience. When we find new life in Christ, we experience a bolt of spiritual growth. We reschedule life around worship and service in a church. We gain a new set of Christian friends. We learn to appreciate the Bible and prayer. We adopt new theological concepts and words. These religious experiences manifest the new spiritual life that has begun to grow at the center of our being. We have become part of Christ's mission to bring the kingdom of God into our lives and, through us, into the broken world.

But as new life in Christ grows, it encounters increasingly stubborn boundaries in our souls. These are pre-established habits of mind, speech, and body that have already shaped our style of living and our sense of who we are. They are reinforced daily in our society. They are ditches and mounds that obstruct our journey with Christ: our opinion of other races, how we comfort ourselves when anxious, what good and evil look like, and the only reasonable way someone would squeeze a tube of toothpaste. We have traced our sense of identity around these and many other such obstacles. They are personal habits influenced by our family, institutions, relationships, entertainment, and social media. They are flawed by what Peter called the corruption in the world because of sinful desire. Yet, since they already establish our path, they seem perfectly normal. It doesn't occur to us that following Christ would challenge how we use toothpaste, even when it is the unnecessary source of friction in a marriage. It also may not occur to us that our views on race or gender might be inconsistent with following Christ. Our mindset and lifestyle feel natural to us, and we could not imagine that Christ would have a different view of how to live.

The initial faith that was sufficient to unite us to Christ, bring us into God's kingdom, and guarantee eternal blessedness is not sufficient to overcome these pre-established boundaries. Why? Because salvation is something Christ entirely accomplishes *for* us, and we receive by faith alone, while transformation is something Christ accomplishes *with* us through the Holy Spirit. Therefore, when we do not supplement our faith wisely and consistently, our growth in Christ hits some inner resistance and goes no further, marking the limit of our spiritual growth. Early success is not sufficient to overcome boundaries we later encounter—The Peter Principle in action.

When I say that simple faith is insufficient to sustain spiritual growth, I mean that faith's inherent and unlimited potential is unrealized without conscious effort. Does a seed have everything necessary to produce a plant? Yes, genetically speaking, but not until soil, water, heat, and sunlight are added appropriately. Abiding in Christ is not passive. A vineyard takes a lot of work for the fruit to grow on its own. Abiding means diligently adding specific qualities to our faith so that God's power can flow from faith to love and bear kingdom fruit.

Peter makes the surprising claim that if the qualities in his list are increasing in us, not only can we grow or even will grow, but it will be impossible for us not to grow kingdom fruit. Re-phrasing the double negative, Peter says that following these dynamics will *inevitably* result in kingdom growth in and through us. He is not bragging about his cleverness; he's praising God for what the Holy Spirit accomplishes when we abide in Christ. Peter sounds like a vinedresser with complete confidence in his vineyard's quality: "Just give the vines what they need, and they'll give you a good crop every time."

When it comes to spiritual growth, The Peter Principle is countered by what I like to call *Peter's Principles*. Discipleship need not be limited to early success, only to permanently plateau when it hits stubborn boundaries. Instead, even settled thoughts, speech patterns, habits, relationships, and spiritual lethargy that once shaped our supposed identity can be reshaped by the Christ-likeness that defines who we were meant to be. This is how Christians grow and Spirit-empowered ministries are made.

§

In the book's next section, we will trace Peter's New Testament journey of discipleship and see how he distills what he experienced into a series of seven steps. Since I believe our discipleship should follow Peter's, I'll also illustrate each step with my experience as best I can. These ordered qualities explain how to abide in Christ, bear fruit that glorifies God, and prove that we are Jesus' disciples.

Discussion Questions for Chapter 4

1. Name some activities that required some training for you to do well.
2. Think of cultivating a vine so that the vine's branches bear fruit.
   a) What requires work? What happens naturally?
   b) Apply this to discipleship.
3. Explain The Peter Principle that is famous in business.
   a) What limits further promotion?
   b) By analogy, what could limit spiritual progress?
4. How do Peter's Principles overcome The Peter Principle when it comes to spiritual growth?

Seven Steps

2 Peter 1:5-7

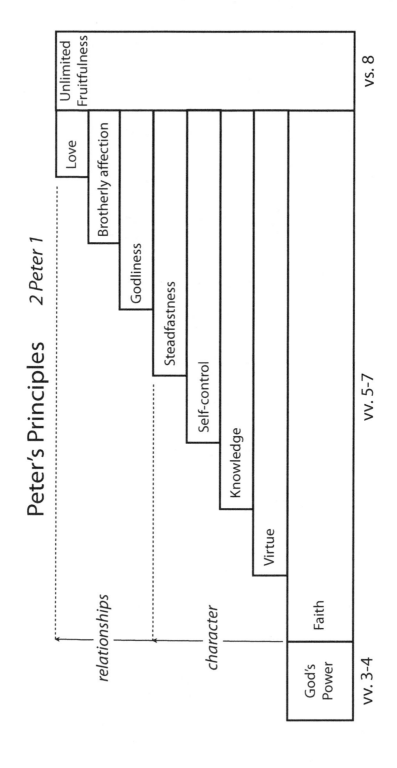

Peter's Principles   *2 Peter 1*

Unlimited Fruitfulness

vs. 8

Love

Brotherly affection

Godliness

Steadfastness

Self-control

Knowledge

Virtue

Faith

relationships

character

vv. 5-7

God's Power

vv. 3-4

50

Chapter 5: Faith

For this very reason, make every effort to supplement your **faith** with virtue, and virtue with knowledge, and knowledge with self-control, and self-control with steadfastness, and steadfastness with godliness, and godliness with brotherly affection, and brotherly affection with love. (2 Peter 1:5-7)

Simon Bar-Jonah was an unlikely candidate for discipleship.

Jewish disciples of that time sought instruction from spiritual masters to follow a particular religious path. Whether scribes or teachers like the Pharisees, they made their way by using their minds. Simon was not dull, but as the owner-operator of a fishing business, he had little time to learn the finer points of religion from a spiritual master. Disciples were expected to spend much time with their masters. They would listen to his teaching and watch him apply it to life's daily challenges and mysteries. But, since no Rabbi was likely to teach from his boat, Simon did not hope to become a disciple anytime soon.

As the eldest, Simon had to manage the family business, but his younger brother Andrew was allowed to indulge his religious interests. So Andrew and his friends trekked down the Jordan River to where the new prophet John was baptizing. While no mention is made of Simon officially following John the Baptist, big brother still made the trip. Perhaps he was also interested, or maybe he just wanted to make sure Andrew wasn't getting into anything over his head. In any case, Simon did not expect to leave his boats for long.

And then Jesus came. John preached some strange but intriguing things about him. Jesus would take away the sins of the world like some sacrificial lamb. The old prophets had spoken of Israel as the bride of the Lord God, but John called Jesus the bridegroom. John said that he saw the Holy Spirit descend from heaven to rest on Jesus and then heard the voice of God declare Jesus to be his Son. John explained that his entire mission was to witness this heavenly recognition of Jesus and prepare the way for him by preaching repentance for the forgiveness of sins. One day, John took Andrew aside and told the earnest young man that Jesus was the one he should follow. Andrew and one of his friends shadowed Jesus at a distance for a few hours. Finally, Jesus invited them to spend some time with him.

It wasn't long before Andrew left to find his brother, Simon. Of course, as the older brother, Simon wanted to evaluate this new teacher Andrew was so excited about. But from the beginning, it was clear that Jesus was evaluating Simon. Perhaps he foresaw in Simon the outworking of an ancient promise because he gave Simon a nickname the fisherman could not possibly appreciate until much later. Jesus said, "You are Simon the son of John? You shall be called Cephas" (John 1:42).

Cephas is Aramaic for "rock." Since the closest thing to a universal language at the time was Greek, the name would soon be exchanged for the Greek word for rock, *Petros*, which is how Simon got the nickname "Peter." I think the modern equivalent of a nickname would sound more like Rocky, but we'll stick with Peter for tradition's sake.

Simon's faith story began when Jesus changed his name. From their very first meeting, it was as if Jesus knew Simon better than Simon knew Simon because Jesus knew Simon's real name. As mentioned in an earlier chapter, Simon's nickname, Peter, would one day tie Jesus and Simon to Daniel's prophecy about the Son of Man and the worldwide expansion of God's kingdom.

Simon did not know that yet. There was so much that Simon/Peter did not yet understand. How did Jesus know what he was talking about? "Lamb of God" was an apparent reference to Temple sacrifices, but how would Jesus become God's lamb? Still, Jesus seemed uniquely connected to God. More than that, Jesus appeared to know Simon's true identity. If Simon indeed was "Peter," he wanted to find out who this Peter was.

§

Faith is not one of Peter's seven steps. We consider it first, however, because all the steps depend upon it.

Jesus calls people to faith in him, and all Christians have stories of how he did that. Some stories parallel that of John the Baptist, who seemed sensitive to Jesus before he was born.[1] Mine was closer to that of the Apostle Paul, who had to be knocked off his horse to get his attention.[2] Several significant episodes marked Peter's story: his first meeting with Jesus, witnessing Jesus' first miracle, confessing Jesus as the Christ, personally receiving the Holy Spirit, and taking the lead when the Holy Spirit inaugurated the Church's worldwide mission.[3]

Therefore, when Peter characterizes faith as the foundation for all discipleship, he cannot point to just one experience and tell us we must have something similar. Instead, he summarizes the message of the gospel. We know that we are right with God and ready to follow Jesus when we believe what Christians are called to believe. Peter defines that faith just before the passage featured in this book:

Simon Peter, a servant and apostle of Jesus Christ, To those who have obtained a faith of equal standing with ours by the righteousness of our God and Savior Jesus Christ: (2 Peter 1:1)

---

[1] Luke 1:15,41.

[2] Acts 9:1-19.

[3] John 2:11; Matthew 16:13-19; John 20:19-23; Acts 1:4-5, 2:1-4.

Regardless of how we encountered Christ, we know we have saving faith when this describes what we believe. So let's look at these two verses in detail, phrase by phrase.

A servant and apostle of Jesus Christ

The kingdom of God has a King, and it is Jesus. Over the centuries, he has appointed leaders for his people, but these leaders are always his servants. He introduced his Church's commission by declaring, "All authority in heaven and on earth has been given to me."[4] His authority, complete and final, is the authority of the Almighty Creator manifested on earth through the incarnate Son of God. This is relevant to the message of salvation because only God has the right to decree the purpose of his creation; only God has the right to critique how we choose to live; and only God can bring us to our senses, deal with our failures, and get us back to accomplishing his original purpose on earth.

Sometimes I desire to tweak the gospel message to suit myself. But the truth concerning salvation is always more wonderful than anything my half-baked ideas can imagine. God communicated this good news by repeatedly intervening in human history. Each time, he raised messengers, called prophets, to explain the significance of what he did, objectively vindicating the credibility of their message through signs and wonders. The last of these unique prophets were disciples Jesus called his apostles, like Simon Peter. God's message to his prophets and apostles was written in the Old and New Testaments.

The one single, coordinated theme of their message is Jesus Christ.[5] The Old Testament is a historical narrative and genealogy of a single family through whom God would renew the earth to his original design, banishing evil and establishing

---

[4] Matthew 28:18.
[5] Luke 24:27; John 5:39.

eternal life.[6] The New Testament identifies the culmination of this genealogy as Jesus.[7] He is *Savior* because he made it possible for us to again take our place as God's image to care for this world. He is *Lord* because he is the single designated authority in the kingdom of God.

Simon Peter gave us the story of Jesus' life through the writer John Mark, who published Peter's memories in the Gospel of Mark. Add Peter's sermons and actions recorded in the Book of Acts and his two letters in the New Testament, and he tells us a great deal about Jesus. His testimony about Jesus, combined with the other apostles, explains the Old Testament and defines the Christian faith.

The Church is faithful to Christ when it is faithful to the original apostles' message. The Apostle John put it this way,

> Let what you heard from the beginning abide in you. If what you heard from the beginning abides in you, then you too will abide in the Son and in the Father. And this is the promise that he made to us—eternal life. (1 John 2:24-25)

Peter begins by reminding us that the gospel is what he and the other apostles appointed by Jesus say it is. That was the job Christ gave them.

Those who have obtained a faith

The word translated as *obtained* literally means to receive something by drawing lots. In the context of Peter's letter, it does not mean faith is by chance but rather that it comes unexpectedly and not as something we earn or cause. People with faith are blessed beyond anything they deserve. It is my experience that Christians feel surprised to be so blessed. Our typical response to obtaining faith in Christ is a grateful, "Why me?"

---

[6] The genealogy is promised in Genesis 3:14-15 and becomes the organizing principle of the Old Testament.

[7] Luke 3:23-38; see also Matthew 1:1-17.

This is not the place to explore the mystery of how divine and human action intertwine in our faith experience. Suffice it to say that God and we are both involved. Jesus described it as suddenly discovering something that most do not recognize:

> The kingdom of heaven is like treasure hidden in a field, which a man found and covered up. Then in his joy he goes and sells all that he has and buys that field.
> Again, the kingdom of heaven is like a merchant in search of fine pearls, who, on finding one pearl of great value, went and sold all that he had and bought it. (Matthew 13:44-46)

I was a committed atheist throughout my youth. I strongly argued against any reference to God in the Maryland State Constitution during a High School exercise in the Annapolis Capitol building. I worked hard from childhood through college to become a rational (read *atheist*) scientist. So how, over five months, did I become a follower of Jesus, willing to devote my entire life to him? I can recount my experience (and would be delighted to do so over coffee), but I cannot fully explain it. It was like unexpectedly recognizing treasure in a field. Why did I suddenly see a fortune in what I formerly saw as a stone, stump, or pile of trash? I don't know.

The Bible describes faith as an awakened spiritual sense. Jesus sometimes healed physical senses like sight or hearing and then went on to teach, saying, "If anyone has ears to hear, let him hear."[8] Using this kind of language from Moses and the prophets, Jesus likened the physical restoration of a sense to a spiritual awakening.[9] It is the sentiment expressed in the hymn *Amazing Grace*, "I once was lost, but now am found, was blind, but now I see."

That awakening of an inner sense that *sees* gospel truth amounts to a personal encounter with Christ. In effect, we recognize Jesus as the key to our purpose when we see that the apostles' message about him is true. What we experience as

---

[8] Matthew 11:3, 15.

[9] Deuteronomy 29:4; Jeremiah 25:4; Ezekiel 12:2.

faith is the real, risen Jesus manifesting himself to us through the gospel.[10] The gospel message that we would otherwise find foolish or offensive (or both) suddenly makes sense.[11] We are involved in the change, we experience this new ability to see, we can describe it but we cannot explain it because we did not cause it.

Does this mean that God draws people to faith regardless of what they want? Not at all. Faith is always a conscious response to God. It responds to something Jesus initiates, as he did with Peter when they first met. The Bible advises anyone interested in finding God to search for him. Jesus said that those who seek are guaranteed to find.[12] This is not because we can discover the truth on our own but because God has chosen to reveal himself through our searching. We must seek him until he finds us.

Faith in the gospel recognizes Jesus himself as the truth of God.[13] Such faith is more expansive than it may first appear because what we believe is true about God ultimately changes how we see reality. C. S. Lewis observed,

> I believe in Christianity as I believe that the sun has risen—not only because I see it, but because by it I see everything else.[14]

Faith in the gospel truly is like a mustard seed. As with Peter, it starts very small and is focused on Jesus. But as we observe in Peter's mature letters, faith grows to create a home for all of life with Christ at the center.[15]

---

[10] John 14:20-23.

[11] A meditation on this can be found in 1 Corinthians 1:18-2:16.

[12] Isaiah 55:6-7; Matthew 7:7-11; see also John 7:17.

[13] John 3:33-36.

[14] C. S. Lewis, "Theology is Poetry," from *They Asked for a Paper - Papers and Addresses*, Geoffrey Bles, London, 1962, pp. 165-166.

[15] Luke 13:13-19.

Faith of equal standing

Salvation is the same for everyone. When Peter mentions "a faith of equal standing with ours," he might have been writing as a Jew to Gentiles, an old man writing to the next generation, or an apostle saying that his standing with God is the same as any other Christian's. In any case, there are no favorite types of people with God. People of any race, age, level of spiritual maturity, or ministry calling have the same standing with God through faith in Christ.

The things that give us higher or lower reputations with each other have no weight with God. Everyone's reputation before God is initially determined by our moral record as God witnessed and remembers it. Whoever wishes to stand on that record may certainly do so and accept the consequences. But for people willing to face their faults and failures before that day, God has provided another way.

When Peter associates our faith with a *standing* with God, he refers to God's acceptance and approval. Only one person has truly and completely earned the right to stand accepted before God.[16] Any hope of having a standing like that involves receiving the gift of sharing what Jesus earned. This is what faith accomplishes and is precisely what it means to be saved. Sharing Jesus' standing puts every believer on an equal status because it is the same status—the standing Christ achieved. In the race of life, everyone initially stands according to how they finish. Through faith, Jesus invites us out of our finish order to stand with him on the winner's platform.

The righteousness of our God and Savior, Jesus Christ

God's approval is tied to righteousness. So perhaps it would be helpful to remember what righteousness means.

Righteousness describes living according to what is right or correct. The English word reflects our notion of *right*-ness, graphically depicted as a right or 90° angle. It describes a

---

[16] Luke 3:21-22.

person whose inner life fits together in all its parts and also aligns with others in healthy relationships. Righteousness affirms the order God designed and our place in it.

Sin rejects God's design, producing a jagged character and ill-fitting relationships. The Bible says that every human being except one has sinned.[17]

When something is broken, it must be either repaired or discarded. Christ came to repair us by preserving our unique personality while ultimately crafting within us a new moral character able to love. Someone who is saved remains the same person yet becomes a radically different person all at the same time. We are not replaced, but we are transformed. Peter didn't replace Simon. Over time, Simon became the Peter he was meant to be.

The only alternative to being repaired is to be discarded. The valley south of Jerusalem is called Gehenna (the Valley of Hinnom). It was associated with Israel's worst idolatry and the fires of human sacrifice.[18] Jeremiah used this valley as a striking image of where the wicked would be cast.[19] Jesus followed Jeremiah in likening the destination of the unsaved to Gehenna. English Bibles translate the specific place name Gehenna with the generic word Hell. That is probably because translators realized that Jesus did not mean the unsaved would be consigned to the valley south of Jerusalem. Like Jeremiah, he meant that those who abandon God would end up exiled to a place like Gehenna, associated with the fires of idolatry and death. Wherever it may be located, no one wants to go to Hell. But when someone refuses to live under God's rule, there is nowhere else to be.

God can lovingly repair us, but ethically, he will always reject unrighteousness. He cannot be both straight and crooked and would not be righteous if he tolerated unrighteousness. At the same time, God does not enjoy

---

[17] Ecclesiastes 7:20; Romans 3:23; Hebrews 4:14-15.
[18] 2 Chronicles 28:3; 33:6.
[19] Jeremiah 7:32; 19:6.

rejecting people he created.[20] The tension between love and justice would seem unsolvable. Nevertheless, the gospel declares that God did solve it by coming to us in Jesus to exchange his accomplished righteousness for our failed attempts.

By arrangement with his Heavenly Father, Jesus died as a kind of flesh-and-blood placeholder on the cross so that all the sin, moral weakness, and wickedness of God's people were collectively counted as his.[21] To speak more personally, God punished my sin while at the same time shielding me from harm by taking on human flesh and absorbing on my behalf the punishment I deserved. Nothing was held back; all the rejection that defines Hell was poured out on the utterly rejected man on the cross. God saw *me* in that man. Praise God, I never felt a thing and never will because Jesus took my place and exchanged his identity for mine on the cross. The Apostle Paul used analogies from the law court (my sentence has been served by someone else) and banking (my debt has been paid by someone else) to explain this. Peter simply repeated what he had been unable to watch:

> He himself bore our sins in his body on the tree, that we might die to sin and live to righteousness. By his wounds you have been healed. For you were straying like sheep, but have now returned to the Shepherd and Overseer of your souls. (1 Peter 2:24-25)

Faith in Jesus creates a spiritual union with him that exchanges our sins for his righteousness. In him, our sin is judged, and in us, his righteousness becomes our new and eternal standing in God's kingdom forever.

By itself, saving faith is not the goal of salvation. Christ did not save me so I can continue forever living in sin. I am destined to be transformed to mirror Christ's character and love. Saving faith is not the goal but rather the means of obtaining what Jesus called eternal life.

---

[20] Ezekiel 18:23,32, 33:11.
[21] 1 Peter 2:24-25.

My story

By the Fall of 1969, something inside me had changed. For the first time, Jesus seemed real to me, and the Bible was making sense. The campus Christian group I had joined sponsored a weekend retreat near Harper's Ferry, Maryland. On a narrow ridge overlooking the river valley, you could see Maryland, Virginia, and West Virginia. The campsite had buildings for food, sleep, activities, and worship. The Chapel was striking, a steeply angled A frame with a wall of glass overlooking the valley. While worshipping, you could gaze through the glass and beyond a towering white cross just outside to see the valley below.

One night, a local pastor tried to explain how God could love sinners. I had been part of this conversation long enough to know he wasn't trying to insult me personally by speaking of my sin. Sinner describes people who don't live as they were meant to because they are disconnected from the Lord. I had difficulty focusing on his message because I struggled to deal with my sin. The offense of taking my Creator for granted and defining life for myself, not to mention how I had slandered Christianity for years, was weighing on my soul.

After the talk, everyone stayed around to enjoy each other's company—everyone except me. I wandered out in what was now late at night and found myself walking into the dark Chapel. Only safety lights glowing, dark and still. Even the glass wall seemed opaque in the darkness. I found the organ, which I didn't know how to turn on, and sat down. Alone in the quiet, I asked aloud, "God, how could you possibly love me?"

At the instant the question left my lips, I heard a *clunk* somewhere in the wall where a timer must have gone off. Instantly, super bright searchlights lit the huge outside cross right in my face. The image was forever etched upon my soul, connecting with what the pastor had said about how God could love sinners ... like me.

The place of faith in Peter's Principles

The Great Commission describes the process of discipleship as three-fold.[22] One verb, make disciples, is explained by three participles. First, we are charged with *going* with the gospel to all nations.[23] Second, we are called to *baptize* and enfold believers in the Church.[24] Third, we are told to *train obedience* to all of Jesus' commands.[25] When the context involves unbelievers, making disciples begins with bringing the gospel to people and, when some believe, enfolding them in the Church. Peter, however, is specifically writing to people who are already members of Christ's Church but have not yet been effectively taught how to obey what Christ commands.[26] As a result, their discipleship has not been completed.

Peter reviews the nature of saving faith to emphasize that discipleship—the training portion—assumes that we already believe. Indeed, the entire sequence Peter lays out depends on the first transition from faith to virtue or aspiration. In other words, saving faith is never something that a Christian can afford to take for granted. Spiritual growth depends on revisiting our faith constantly. The passion to follow Jesus is kindled only when our appreciation of God's amazing grace overflows. Every step forward in our walk with Christ depends on our soul responding to what Christ has already done for us.

Of course, while Peter is gracious in addressing Christians who are not growing spiritually (verse 9), there is always the possibility that a confessing Christian cannot grow because they do not believe what they confess. Saving faith is not only a matter of confession, which we can outwardly observe, but also trust in the heart, which we cannot directly observe.[27] By declaring that faith is necessary for discipleship, Peter gently

---

[22] Matthew 28:18-20.

[23] Luke 24:45-47.

[24] 1 Corinthians 12:13.

[25] John 14:21; 1 Thessalonians 1:8-9.

[26] 2 Peter 1:1,9.

[27] Romans 10:9-10.

encourages confessing Christians and their shepherds to discern whether saving faith exists. If it does not, then discipleship training cannot be effective. In that case, it would be better to encourage a humble search for God in the Lord Jesus.

Saving faith is the prerequisite to seeking my intended identity. Through faith, I realize I don't have to make myself a different person for God to accept me. God has accepted me in Christ and already created the seed of a new me. I want to be discipled so I can find out who this new person is.

Saving faith in the pursuit of Christ's mission

Throughout history, there have always been leaders who use the name of Jesus for their own kingdom vision. Peter warned us.

> But false prophets also arose among the people, just as there will be false teachers among you, who will secretly bring in destructive heresies, even denying the Master who bought them, bringing upon themselves swift destruction. And many will follow their sensuality, and because of them the way of truth will be blasphemed. And in their greed they will exploit you with false words. Their condemnation from long ago is not idle, and their destruction is not asleep. (2 Peter 2:1-3)

Religious and political movements, institutions, and even some previously faithful churches have operated under the name of Christ while abandoning the biblical basics of saving faith. They exchange Jesus' mission for something else. Many seek to do good, though Peter warns of mercenary motives and holy-looking fronts for sensuality. Without saving faith, they are not part of God's kingdom and, therefore, cannot build it.[28] By misrepresenting God, they may even hinder the kingdom's expansion.[29]

---

[28] Matthew 7:21-23.
[29] Mathew 23:15.

Jesus' mission is to bring the whole earth into the righteousness and love of God's rule. He will complete that task when he returns. Until then, he brings individuals into God's kingdom through the gift of a new identity linked to him and received through faith. His reputation is ours in the Father's sight,[30] and his Spirit lives in our spirit and body.[31]

Discipleship builds on that faith by training us how to unwrap our new identity and join Jesus in his mission.

§

Every Christian has a story of how Jesus found them or how they came to faith. Your account will differ from mine. Your specific details are deeply treasured memories and valuable when discussing your faith with others. But what matters most is not how you came to believe but what you believe. Do you trust Christ to share with you his pure and perfect relationship with God?

If you do, you must sense that your identity is now connected to Jesus. Simon felt it the day Jesus changed his name, and he spent the rest of his life discovering who he was meant to be. A mature Peter will tell us how we can do the same. On the foundation of our faith, he teaches us to add seven qualities that bring the kingdom of God into our lives and through our lives to others.

---

[30] Romans 3:21-26.
[31] Romans 8:9-11; 1 Corinthians 6:19-20.

Discussion Questions for Chapter 5

1. Do you know the original meaning of your first, middle, and last name? Perhaps you could look it up online or in a book.
   a) Do you think it accurately describes everything God made you to be?
   b) How would you feel if God told you your name was something else—that you are meant to be a person who thinks, feels, and acts somewhat differently than you have learned to do?
2. Discuss how salvation is related to the righteousness of Jesus Christ.
3. What is significant about the way faith is positioned in Peter's list?

Chapter 6: Virtue

For this very reason, make every effort to **supplement your faith with virtue**, and virtue with knowledge, and knowledge with self-control, and self-control with steadfastness, and steadfastness with godliness, and godliness with brotherly affection, and brotherly affection with love. (2 Peter 1:5-7)

To Simon's surprise, Jesus went with them on their trip back home from the Jordan River, adopting their hometown of Capernaum as his base of operations. Simon was delighted to host this brilliant new Rabbi in his house. Still, having Jesus as a guest was one thing; discipleship was another. Discipleship seemed impossible for this fisherman since it was hardly likely that any Master would teach from his boat. Until one day, that's what happened.

In what was probably a first for any Rabbi, Jesus asked to teach from Simon's fishing boat! While a large crowd gathered on a suitable shoreline, Jesus created an ad hoc amphitheater to address them. Working next to or behind Jesus, Simon kept the boat oriented. Yet Simon was invisible to the crowd; all eyes were fixed and focused on Jesus. This gave Simon the unusual perspective of discretely seeing people exactly as Jesus saw them.

This is the only time on record that Jesus taught from a boat. The crowd assumed he set it up that way for them. But given what he did immediately after teaching, he probably chose the arrangement specifically for Simon. He wanted Simon to see the good news of the kingdom from God's perspective, which is to say, from Jesus' perspective. Looking over the Master's shoulder, Simon saw what only Jesus could see.

People came to Jesus for different reasons, but most were desperate. Simon looked at the people he knew from town and others just like them and saw physical pain, moral bondage, spiritual confusion, and despair. He was used to seeing resignation that mixed bits of happiness into years of labor, always ending in a grave. But as Jesus spoke, Simon saw something that perhaps he had never seen before: hope. Hope was blazing in those whom Jesus had already touched, already healed, and the same flame was being kindled in many others. It was as if, in speaking, Jesus breathed life into them. Jesus talked about the coming of God's kingdom, and in the faces of those who began to hope, Simon could *see* it coming. It was as if Jesus *was* the kingdom of God among them.

Simon knew what it was like to be in the crowd. Like them, he was familiar with his sin and shortcomings through the Law that spoke of God's will. And like them, he saw in Jesus' healing and words hope for restoration to how things— and people—were supposed to be.

But this time, Simon was not in the crowd. Instead, he looked virtually through the eyes of the one who brought tangible hope to others. He saw and felt what the kingdom of God could mean, not just for him but anyone who welcomed the good news. Could a human being ever do anything more wonderful than what Jesus was doing? Simon's heart must have been ready to burst. No one else could do what Simon saw Jesus doing.

As the crowd dispersed, Jesus did not want to be put ashore. Instead, he asked the fisherman to put his nets over one more time, knowing that hard work through the previous night had yielded nothing. Jesus had worked miracles, but what could he expect from a simple, sinful fisherman? Yet, as his nets filled to breaking under an enormous haul of fish,

Simon realized that a miracle was happening *in his hands*. Jesus not only could do the impossibly wonderful but also do it *through others*.

Even so, surely Jesus would want someone less rough and sinful. So Simon knelt in his boat in anguish as a sinner who knew himself to be unworthy. But Jesus did not react in disgust. He did not correct him or explain the mysteries of salvation. Instead, artfully linking the miracle of gospel hope to the one accomplished through Peter's hands, he said to Simon, "Do not be afraid; from now on you will be catching men" (Luke 5:8-10).

There had been no job interview. No assessment of qualifications. No analysis of potential. Jesus simply called Simon to work with him for the kingdom of God. The fisherman would ponder what happened for the rest of his life. Jesus called Simon to embrace a life so different that it deserved the new name Christ had given him earlier, Peter. He had no words to explain it, but with Jesus in his life, Simon, or Peter, was becoming a new person. He was the same man, only different. He would spend the rest of his life discovering and marveling at the difference. He would continue to see the faces Jesus saw and function as Jesus' hands to draw them into God's kingdom.

> And when they had brought their boats to land, they left everything and followed him. (Luke 5:11)

Simon had no idea where Jesus would take him; he just wanted to follow. He wanted more of what he experienced that day with Jesus, and he wanted it more than he ever wanted anything. So he quickly arranged for the business to continue indefinitely without him because Simon Peter was ready to follow Jesus.

§

Faith in Christ is the launching pad for discipleship. Launch Complex 39 at Cape Canaveral sent up all the Apollo and Space Shuttle flights. Its concrete hardstand covers more than 125,000 square feet with a Fixed Service Structure over 347 feet tall. Just one of its two flame deflectors weighed one and a half million pounds. It had to be substantial to handle the immense exhaust of a Saturn rocket. Like the Launch complex, only faith that's based 100% on God's grace in Christ is strong enough to support discipleship.

What, then, is the force anticipated by such a platform that can lift off and enable us to fly as the Christ-like people we were designed to be? Peter calls that motive force *virtue*.

Virtue translates *aretē*, an important Greek word referring to moral excellence. It is the word Peter used earlier in verses 3-4 when he spoke of life and godliness, glory, and *excellence*. The term describes the highest ideal of goodness, the aspiration to be a morally good human being. Of the billions of people throughout history, only one person has been truly and perfectly good. As his disciples, our goal is to become like him. By describing virtue as the first thing we must make every effort to add to our faith, Peter implies that such aspiration is not always burning; we must regularly work to ignite it.

A passion for Christ's virtue is not spontaneous, even for believers, because it is not how we were wired from birth. We are born with a stubborn predisposition to distrust God and even lay aside the conscience he gave us to get what we want. We are born morally broken and prone to fear, discontent, self-pity, envy, and bitterness. Goodness does not grow well in such soil. What we understand as goodness is always linked to what we believe about God. Mankind will not acknowledge the Living God and defines goodness by our own measures. Our efforts are so inconsistent and disappointing that our understanding of goodness is jaded and confused.

Jesus, however, makes true goodness recognizable. Most would say that Jesus is godly, meaning that his virtue illustrates what many imagine God to be like. But faith in Christ turns that around. Believing Christ to be God in human form, we realize that *God is like Jesus*. This is life-changing because we no longer have to wonder what goodness is. We see it in Jesus. We no longer have to wonder what God thinks of us or whether we can trust him. When we see that God is like Jesus, we understand that God has exercised his perfect goodness for our eternal good. If God is like Jesus, then God spares no expense and makes any personal sacrifice to deal with our needs and afflictions.

MY FATHER,
  Enlarge my heart, warm my affections,
    open my lips,
    supply words that proclaim 'Love lustres
    at Calvary.'
  There grace removes my burdens and heaps them
    on thy Son,
    made a transgressor, a curse, and sin for me;
  There the sword of thy justice smote the man,
    thy fellow;
  There thy infinite attributes were magnified,
    and infinite atonement was made;
  There infinite punishment was due,
    and infinite punishment was endured.
  Christ was all anguish that I might be all joy,
    cast off that I might be brought in,
    trodden down as an enemy
      that I might be welcomed as a friend,
    surrendered to hell's worst
      that I might attain heaven's best,
    stripped that I might be clothed,
    wounded that I might be healed,
    athirst that I might drink,
    tormented that I might be comforted,
    made a shame that I might inherit glory,
    entered darkness that I might have eternal light.
  My Saviour wept that all tears might be wiped
    from my eyes,
    groaned that I might have endless song,
    endured all pain that I might have unfading health,
    bore a thorny crown that I might have
    a glory-diadem,
    bowed his head that I might uplift mine,
    experienced reproach that I might receive welcome,
    closed his eyes in death that I might gaze

on unclouded brightness,
 expired that I might for ever live.
O Father, who spared not thine only Son that thou
   mightest spare me,
All this transfer thy love designed and
   accomplished;
Help me to adore thee by lips and life.
O that my every breath might be ecstatic praise,
 my every step buoyant with delight, as I see my
   enemies crushed,
 Satan baffled, defeated, destroyed,
 sin buried in the ocean of reconciling blood,
 hell's gates closed, heaven's portal open.
Go forth, O conquering God, and show me
 the cross, mighty to subdue, comfort and save.
("Love Lustres at Calvary"[1])

The power of poetry like this is amplified when lovingly paired with music. Artfully used, music saturates the soul with God's goodness. Songs tune our spirit to resonate with God's Spirit, echoing the truth of his goodness back to him. Worshiping through music creates a focus enabling the mind and heart to lay aside other distractions. Singing to God together or alone drenches us in the joy of who God is. One of the most powerful ways to renew spiritual aspiration is to let well-crafted Christian songs and hymns have their way with us.[2] We are so blessed to have a wealth of recorded music at our fingertips. We can use it whenever we wish to give our full attention to truths that rise to God and lift us along with them. I strive to begin and end each day by engaging with one of my growing list of worship songs. It is the simplest thing I do to keep my aspiration for Christ-likeness fresh.

Of course, there are many other ways to privately revive our desire to share Christ's goodness: intimate prayer, worship offered in the beauty of creation, meditation upon Bible passages, or reviewing our past journey with him. Some of us

---

[1] *Valley of Vision*, Arthur Bennet, ed., Banner of Truth Trust, Edinburgh, 1975, pp. 42-43.
[2] Ephesians 5:14-21; Colossians 3:12-17.

find fresh passion when we talk about him with others. The important thing is to regularly celebrate how Christ is worthy to be praised. Meditating on Christ and his gospel kindles aspiration for a life filled, guided, and empowered by his goodness. The Christian Church meets weekly to celebrate this gospel, proclaiming our best understanding from the pulpit and our best adoration in prayer, song, and sacrament. Participating in that celebration of saving faith rekindles our desire to be like him.

When we do not regularly celebrate Christ in his gospel greatness, we drift away into legalism, pride, or indifference. We get lost in programs and politics. None of those things will motivate us to imitate his goodness. When Christians attempt to build God's kingdom without constantly refreshed aspiration for Christ's virtue, we tend to pursue our kingdoms, not his.

We see in Jesus' humanity the best possible human being, and we thrive when we purposefully wrap our will around God's will embodied in him. Childlike faith in the gospel saves us forever because salvation is all Christ's doing but for us to overcome the gravity of sin requires something more. We need the powerful engine of aspiration.

Aspiration to share Christ's virtue is delicious when fresh, but it has a short shelf-life. When my wife, Micki, buys freshly sliced ham or cooks some hard-boiled eggs, she puts them in the fridge with a label noting when they were purchased or prepared. Then, after an appropriate number of days, she disposes of whatever is left. A given supply will not last long. Divine manna only lasted a day. Our Sabbath celebrations renew spiritual aspiration, but the emotional vigor doesn't last more than a week. Christians who neglect to regularly supplement faith with the aspiration to live like Jesus will lack the motivation to move through the remaining six steps that Peter lays out. Discipleship begins and thrives with a passion to be like Jesus.

Perpetually overwhelmed

America is experiencing a crisis of identity, both national and personal. Rejecting the Creator God, we think to find freedom in defining ourselves. But this freedom is a trap, enslaving us to ignorantly short-sighted whims. Our identity shrinks to whichever opinions are thrust into our faces. We imagine ourselves as better people because we identify with Blue instead of Red or Red rather than Blue. The latest viral craze can alter our sense of identity. The spiritual poverty of America has never been more evident. The louder we shout our opinions, the more they echo from empty souls. We have no idea where we came from, who we are, or where we are going.

Christian disciples discover what it means to no longer be lost, trying to define themselves. Instead, we are finding who we are meant to be in Christ's character and love. Once united to Christ by faith, a new identity takes root. We see the lives we used to lead as aberrations of what God designed. In Christ, we see what we are destined to become. Of course, we will explore the delightful details and quirks of our personalities and talents, for God loves extravagant variety. But we are all meant to share Jesus' worthy character and healthy relationships, for he is the perfect human being.

To anyone who, like Peter, is painfully aware of their moral shortcomings, the goal of Christ-likeness seems impossible—until, again like Peter, they realize that Jesus can perform miracles of grace in and through us. Whenever we rediscover that Christ is alive and remember what he can do, the wonder of our calling seems too good to be true.

> As they were talking about these things, Jesus himself stood among them ... "See my hands and my feet, that it is I myself. Touch me, and see" ... And while *they still disbelieved for joy* and were marveling, he said to them, "Have you anything here to eat?" (Luke 24:36-41, *emphasis added*)

For just a moment, when they encountered the risen Christ, those first disciples were too stunned to take it in. Every Christian knows how they felt because we feel the same thing over and over whenever a fresh encounter with Christ awakens us from spiritual lethargy. We become freshly overwhelmed that Jesus is alive and momentarily hesitate to put our weight on that faith. To know the risen Jesus seems too marvelous and incredible in a world as broken and hopeless as ours.

If Jesus is alive, then *everything is different*. Faith in Christ is not just about faith in Christ. It's also about everything true because of it. Faith in Christ means that the saving power of God has been unleashed in the world. Faith in Christ means I have a vast spiritual family of real people on their way to becoming whole. Faith in Christ means that I will never, ever be alone. Faith in Christ means that my every failure and shame—past, present, and future—is forever buried in his tomb. Faith in Christ means that my aching body will one day be healed, and my self-destructive habits are doomed. Faith in Christ makes my worth independent of the opinion of people who are as broken as I am. Faith in Christ makes me part of a project overarching all human history. Faith in Christ guarantees an eternal life that is worth living. Faith in Christ makes me God's friend.

Whenever we see Jesus afresh by faith, we see our new identity freshly washed and ready for us to put on. When such aspiration is rekindled, there is that exquisite instant of disbelief, born not of doubt but astounded joy.

My story

I was first asked to preach a few months after I confessed Christ from atheism. I wish I could sit down with each reader and recount the story. It was equal parts hilarious and humiliating. I treated the event as The Glenn Show. After I crashed and burned, I could almost hear Jesus speak out loud as he warned me that if I ever again tried to promote myself while handling his Word, he would see to it that I experienced that same level of humiliation. The experience was so real I trembled.

And I wept for joy because I realized that the risen and living Jesus cared about what I did. He wanted me to represent him well, working alongside him to bring the kingdom of God into the world. He insisted that I behave, but he wanted to work with me! For years, I had searched for a dream big enough to live for, and what I found was not a dream but an opportunity to serve the one who has given all mankind life and breath and everything.[3]

From that moment on, I have looked to Jesus every day as my Hero. He always understands a situation better than I do. His feelings are always pure and perfectly targeted. He is not afraid of anything and always knows what to do when the time is right.

I aspire to be his sidekick. The sidekick is faithful and helpful. He provides comic relief with his foibles but is dearly loved by the Hero, who always looks out for him while graciously (and creatively) finding ways for him to contribute to the Hero's adventure. Over 40 years of pastoring a church and a family, I have learned never to approach any challenge independently. I wait for my Hero, and I follow him in. I expect him to make the difference, and I contribute where I can. Jesus promises to keep me from stumbling all the way to the heavenly throne, where he will present me blameless before the presence of God's glory with great joy.[4] The Heavenly Father will then see before him his only beloved son and, beside him, a former sidekick who has graduated to become a hero himself. That's how competent Jesus is!

As I write this, I find myself, just for a moment, disbelieving for joy.

The place of virtue in Peter's Principles

I was properly trained to understand that salvation is not based on my emotions or feelings. While finding Christ was an

---

[3] Acts 17:25.
[4] Jude 24-25.

emotional experience for me, I realize that my salvation does not depend on how I felt at the time. I was, am, and shall always be saved by simple trust in who Jesus is, what he did, what he is doing now, and what he will do.

As I ponder Peter's Principles, however, I see that I was not taught the importance of ongoing spiritual motivation. An emotional desire to become like Jesus and join him in his mission is critical to following him. Without it, Bible knowledge becomes academic and lifeless, and self-control (obedience) becomes pretense because it does not flow from the heart. The aspiration for virtue—to be reshaped around Jesus' goodness—provides the motivation that propels everything else. That is why virtue is prominent among Peter's elements. It is the first thing we must regularly add to faith. This is so important: every successive element of discipleship depends on the motive force of moral aspiration.

It can be easy to forget this as we move through Peter's seven steps. Having experienced a passion for following Christ in the past, we will be tempted to check that off our list and focus on other matters. But that is not how these steps work. All steps must function simultaneously for each to be supported from below and provide support for what lies above. In other words, no further progress can be made whenever the aspiration to share Christ's goodness is not fresh. Even if we perfectly understand Peter's entire process, we always need adequate motivation to keep moving forward.

Virtue in the pursuit of Christ's mission

Christians can be induced to do religious things for many reasons. But guilt, shame, pride, social pressure, self-righteousness, and religious habit will not accomplish much. While such motivations may sustain programs, they cannot build a kingdom where the Living God rules. Did Jesus labor for his Father's kingdom out of guilt? Pride? Social pressure? If I want to work with him, I cannot sit in those shadows. The curtains of my heart must be thrown open to bask in the goodness of God that I see in Christ.

Consider this testimony from the autobiography of George Mueller:

> It has recently pleased the Lord to teach me a truth, irrespective of human instrumentality, as far as I know, the benefit of which I have not lost, though now, while preparing the fifth edition for the press, more than fourteen years have since passed away. The point is this: I saw more clearly than ever that the first great and primary business to which I ought to attend every day was, to have my soul happy in the Lord.
>
> The first thing to be concerned about was not how much I might serve the Lord, how I might glorify the Lord; but how I might get my soul into a happy state, and how my inner man might be nourished.
>
> For I might seek to set the truth before the unconverted, I might seek to benefit believers, I might seek to relieve the distressed, I might in other ways seek to behave myself as it becomes a child of God in this world; and yet, not being happy in the Lord, and not being nourished and strengthened in my inner man day by day, all this might not be attended to in a right spirit.[5]

Mueller illustrates a truth about emotions that seems unintuitive to the modern mind. Emotions can be cultivated. Feelings can indeed spring up like weeds without any planning or intent on our part. But they can also be intentionally sown, fertilized, and tended. The Apostle Paul taught that emotions could be consciously developed, and disciples need to be trained in doing this.[6] Peter tells us that spiritual growth falters without a cultivated passion for finding oneself in Jesus' goodness.

§

---

[5] *The Life of Trust, the Autobiography of George Mueller*, Ichthus Publications, 2016, Kindle edition.

[6] Philippians 4:4-9.

Where the aspiration to share Christ's virtue is fresh, the soul is eager to continue its spiritual journey. We only need to know which way to go. This takes us to the next step.

Discussion Questions for Chapter 6

1. Can you think of anyone from childhood who inspired you to become like them?
2. What inspired Peter to follow Jesus?
3. What do you think of the entry in George Mueller's autobiography? (Feel free to look back and read it again.)
4. What did it mean for the disciples to "disbelieve for joy" when they first saw the resurrected Christ?
   a) Have you ever felt like that?
   b) If this kind of motivation is necessary in order to progress in discipleship, how might you regularly cultivate it?

Chapter 7: Knowledge

> For this very reason, make every effort to supplement your faith with virtue, **and virtue with knowledge**, and knowledge with self-control, and self-control with steadfastness, and steadfastness with godliness, and godliness with brotherly affection, and brotherly affection with love. (2 Peter 1:5-7)

After Peter's unforgettable day on his boat with Jesus, the next few months were an exciting blur. People started to seek out the Master. They needed medical help. They needed emotional support. They needed spiritual direction. They needed Jesus, who was always there for them, giving much more than they hoped. And because Jesus was living with Peter, that meant that to find Jesus, they had to come to Peter's house.

Peter continued to unobtrusively see Jesus' impact as he had in the boat. People gathered at Peter's home. People at the entrance. People inside—some ripping open his roof to get in. Peter had no power to help any of them, but he was hosting Jesus, and somehow, that meant hosting the kingdom of God. We don't know how Peter's wife felt, but the fact that Jesus gently healed her mother must have softened and intrigued her. Much later, she would join her husband in following Jesus into many other homes.[1]

---

[1] 1 Corinthians 9:5.

There were no classes as we know them. Peter experienced discipleship by listening and watching. All he had to do was to host Jesus as the Master dealt with misery and sin, healing and hope, fame and conflict, blessing and thanksgiving. The theology was profound but hardly academic. Jesus' teaching described what is true, and his life illustrated what he taught. It was an exciting learning time, all within the familiar contours of Peter's daily routine.

Life took on a new cadence. After hours of dealing with needs ranging from simple disease to demonic compulsions, the crowd settled to drink in Jesus' teaching. His brand of gentle authority was unique. He spoke of a way of life fueled by trust in God. He talked of meaning, purpose, and belonging. Jesus taught in a way that made people think. He used parables and illustrations from whatever was at hand, letting the hearer discover the connections and decide where they fit into his stories. Jesus taught the Old Testament like an author explaining what he intended. Moses, the Prophets, and the Psalms all came to life. In Jesus, the Living God lived and breathed in their midst.

§

From the first time we sense the yearning to follow Jesus, we repeatedly face the question of what following Christ means. Passion must come first, but passion is not sufficient. Without accurate knowledge, we will get lost. Discipleship falters when religious passions are misdirected. This can be due to innocent ignorance,[2] misplaced confidence in unhealthy teachers,[3] or a stubborn commitment to wrong ideas.[4] The Apostle Paul lamented over Pharisees who used to be his colleagues:

---

[2] Acts 19:1-2.
[3] 2 Timothy 3:1-7.
[4] 2 Timothy 2:16-18.

> Brothers, my heart's desire and prayer to God for them is that they may be saved. For I bear them witness that they have a zeal for God, but not according to knowledge. (Romans 10:1–2)

If we are to follow Jesus, we need to know the way. The path travels through the kingdom of God's rule toward the destination of God's glory. A crayon treasure map is not enough, but neither is GPS directions to God's heavenly throne if we are bound and determined to go to Vermont instead. We must be willing to follow in Jesus' steps to where Jesus is going.

The religious passion of the Pharisees fueled a fruitless quest for self-righteousness. They were not alone. Throughout Western history, the banner of Christ has been enthusiastically waved over many misguided enterprises and naive ideologies, sometimes religious, sometimes philosophical, and sometimes political. Discipleship teaches how to couple aspiration for Christ's virtue with accurate knowledge of God's will.

The problem is that we are naturally much more interested in our will than in his.

Sherpa or Shepherd?

The Sherpa are Tibetans, most famous to Westerners as guides for intrepid adventurers who yearn to scale imposing mountains. Mountain climbers hire Sherpa as guides, tell them where they want to go and expect help getting there.

Shepherds care for sheep. For the sheep's benefit, a shepherd guides sheep to where he knows they need to go, protecting them, retrieving them, and healing them as necessary.

Is the Living God a Sherpa or a Shepherd to his people? It is stunning how often we treat him as a Sherpa, hired on when we want to move, and expected to help us get to where we want to go. But the biblical reality is that God is our Shepherd. He guides us continually, whether we ask him to or not. He guides us to where he wants us to be, regardless of where we want to go. He will retrieve us when we wander off on what we imagine is a better path, whether or not we want to be found. He will even lead us through the valley of death's shadow because that is the way to finally arrive home.

Christians often think that finding God's will guides us to our goals. What is the best job? Who is the best marriage partner? Will I prosper more if I invest in this or commit to that? But perhaps we are not always searching for what God gives:

> The secret things belong to the LORD our God, but the things that are revealed belong to us and to our children forever, that we may do all the words of this law. (Deuteronomy 29:29)

The Living God knows everything. He knows all that is happening at this moment, all that happened in the past, and all that will happen in the future.[5] The God of the Bible is unlike any imaginary god in that he created everything that exists other than himself—all matter and energy, space and time, and everything else we have yet to discover. God cares about all he created. Therefore, the best way forward must be best not only for me but also for all those around me and all those around them, tomorrow, the day after that, and all eternity. It must best accomplish God's eternal purposes for all his creation. So when we ask to know which option before us is the best, we are asking for a massive data dump. To casually ask for such godlike knowledge is highly presumptuous and would be ridiculously impossible for us to process.

But can't God reveal the result of all that computation applied only to what I'm interested in? He could, of course, but why would he? Do we need such knowledge to do what's right? Do you want your children to ask you to tell them everything they are supposed to do, even as they grow into adulthood and beyond? What would be the value of loving God with all our heart, mind, and strength if we never

---

[5] Ecclesiastes 3:11; Isaiah 46:8-10; Revelation 22:13.

developed our heart or mind or strength to do what he has already told us is right?

Phrasing it this way immediately puts a spotlight on the real issue: we are more interested in God's help to accomplish our goals than pursuing his goal to make us like his only beloved Son. *God's will for us is to live like Jesus* because Jesus embodies everything God created human beings to be. If we seek God's will, that's what we will find. The kind of knowledge we want to exploit remains secret because we don't need it. What we need to know is what God has already abundantly revealed.

God has revealed his will

God's revelation of his will is not at all sparse; we call it his law. Biblical law includes God's commandments, specific cases, general principles, and historical illustrations. It comes in poetry and prose, memorable one-liners, and whole life histories traced for our education. It engages the heart with compelling stories and imprints itself unforgettably on the mind in apocalyptic panoramas. Most broadly defined, God's law refers to everything he has revealed in the Bible about who he is and how he wants us to be like him. Ultimately, God's law is summarized in the gospel accounts and apostolic explanations of Jesus Christ. God wants us to be like Jesus. That is his will for us. That is his guidance.

Every decision in life requires knowledge specific to its context, of course. But in every decision, the most critical knowledge is what God has revealed as his moral will for our lives. That never changes, and that always takes precedence. Consider this familiar passage:

> Trust in the LORD with all your heart, and do not lean on your own understanding. In all your ways acknowledge him, and he will make straight your paths. (Proverbs 3:5-6)

To not lean on our understanding does not mean setting aside our intelligence! It means relying on God to speak through his Word to explain his design and intelligently embracing what he says over all other value and purpose claims. When we act on that knowledge, we travel the way he wants us to go, which Psalm 23 calls "paths of righteousness for his name's sake." God's guidance doesn't always tell us specifically what to do, but we don't need such direction. If we choose to live according to God's revealed will, and he has something special in mind for us that we can't possibly know, he will undoubtedly make sure to "make our paths straight" to lead us there.

The temptation for a Christian is to agree with all this in theory but then set the law off to one side as irrelevant to what I'm seeking at the moment. "Yes, God wants me to be good. I know that. But the law of God doesn't tell me which job offer to take, and that's what is important to me right now." Indeed, God's Word does not tell me which job offer to take, but such questions are never the most important. If I approach my career without a clear focus on living as the man or woman God created me to be, my career will not be well-founded. But if I focus on who I am in Christ as I consider a career, I will follow close behind Jesus instead of wandering off and getting lost. If my heart is Christ's and he has a particular job in mind for me, he will do whatever it takes to guide me to it as a good Shepherd.

Some believe that living by faith involves asking God for his secret will until we get an inner feeling that he has. But we actually lay faith aside when we insist on knowing the outcome of a choice when God has already shown the path of righteousness he wants us to follow. Living by faith means pursuing the character and love of Christ revealed in the Scriptures and believing that the Lord will use our obedience to guide us.

God's will is so much bigger

In verse 3 of our theme text, Peter says that God's promised power "pertains to life and godliness, through the knowledge of him who called us to his own glory and excellence." If this is God's destination for us, then his guidance is much more comprehensive than helping me choose between options I have already pre-defined. The knowledge I need to follow Jesus is not limited to things I happen to be concerned about. If we open our hearts and minds, the knowledge of God revealed in the Bible will direct us in every part of life.

A clear biblical example of this involves King Solomon. When God asked him what favor he most wanted, Solomon said he wanted wisdom to lead well because he was too young to know what that entailed. The Lord was so pleased with this request that he gave Solomon insight like none other. We don't know what specific issues intimidated the young Solomon, but the Bible details how God gave him much more wisdom than he expected: justice in government, leadership in public works, a prosperous economy, and success in music, literature, and natural science. Solomon received wisdom to apply the knowledge of God in every aspect of civilization.[6]

The knowledge craved by Christ-like aspiration may, at first, only relate to a few matters of personal interest, but it keeps expanding. Ultimately, it opens up the entire Cultural Mandate and Great Commission, enabling us to function as God's image and act in his likeness. When we stop relying on our own understanding and instead follow what God has already revealed of Christ's character and love, he will guide us to all the places he wants us to go.

My story

In 1972, I was finishing my undergraduate degree. My parents had worked hard to pay my college costs and were proud of my achievements. But Christ had recently called me, and my life had changed. I announced that I was changing course and hoped to go to seminary. My non-religious parents were dismayed that I was throwing away a promising career in science to pursue, of all things, religion. It was a sensitive and negative topic around the house.

In those days, I sought the Lord for guidance about seminary. When should I go? Did God want me to head there

---

[6] 1 Kings 3-4.

right away, or did he want me to take time to mature in my faith, save up money for tuition, etc.? I asked God to guide me, but no specific answer was apparent.

After several weeks, I made what turned out to be a life-changing decision to focus on what I *did* know about God's will instead of what I *didn't* know. I went immediately to the Ten Commandments and, given the tension in my home, felt drawn to the fifth one about honoring my father and mother.

My Dad was about to retire from a demanding job with the FAA and wanted to start a second career in wedding and portrait photography. Pondering the Fifth Commandment, I realized that my quest for guidance had thus far been all about what I wanted. I realized that wasn't particularly Christ-like. I knew my way around a camera and realized that the right thing for me to do was to volunteer a year or two to help Dad start up his new business and then go to seminary later. So that's what I told my parents. Mom and Dad didn't respond immediately and said they would think about it.

I expected to immediately regret that decision because it wasn't what I wanted to do. Strangely, though, I realized that if this was the will of my God, then it *was* what I wanted to do.

One of my fondest memories about my parents was our following conversation a few weeks later. They came to me together, and I remember what they said as if it were yesterday: "We don't know what happened to you, Glenn, but whatever it is, is good." They told me they thought I should go directly to seminary, and they volunteered to pay my tuition!

I asked God for knowledge of his will about seminary and discovered that I already had knowledge of his will, and it wasn't about seminary. It involved my parents. But it was not ultimately about my parents, either; it was about living like Jesus. I learned that knowledge of God's Word weaves all of life together. When I obeyed what I knew was God's will, even though it didn't seem related to my concern, he made my path straight. He can do that. He is God.

The truth about God's law

Many Christians are burdened with the misunderstanding that God's law was a failed idea that God abandoned when he sent Jesus. It is true that the ceremonial laws in the Old Testament have been fulfilled in Jesus and are no longer in force. It is also true that ancient Israel's national laws were linked to the Lord being their King; they do not directly apply to any other nation. But God's moral law concerning right and wrong outlines God's character. It never changes and always serves as the model for our character.

When the New Testament says that we are free from the law, it means being free from its curse. Christ absorbed the condemnation we deserve for breaking God's law. But salvation then turns God's moral law into the law of the Spirit, motivating me to obey God because I want to rather than because I have to.[7] Since love is the ultimate summary of the law, the law must unpack how to love.[8]

We'll look more at obedience in the next chapter. Right now, my point is that I already have knowledge of God's will for my life if I have access to scriptural teaching. He wants me to live like his Son, who embodied God's biblical revelation. If that is not what I'm seeking, I will not walk in God's will, regardless of which options I choose. But, on the other hand, if I strive to live like his Son and take his Word as my guide, I will walk in his will every day, whichever option I choose. And if he has a particular path for me in mind—job, spouse, or whatever—he will make that option both clear and available, even unavoidable, if necessary. That's how a Shepherd leads sheep.

We may start to follow the Lord as children would follow. Our application of the law is rudimentary: do this, and don't do that. But the Scriptures make it clear that the Lord wants us to develop a mature understanding of his mind, confident that his hopes and dreams for us are much greater than the

---

[7] Romans 8:2.
[8] Mark 12:28-34; Romans 13:8-10.

fantasies we imagine for ourselves.[9] As we mature, we realize that God's law goes beneath behavior to the heart. It values what God values, thinks as he thinks, and feels as he feels. This pulls down the fences we've put up to contain God's will to our immediate interests and opens up the kingdom of God to all my life and all that my life touches. If we do not care about manifesting Christ in a situation, then God still loves us, but he is not especially interested in our choices. However, if we want to manifest Christ in this world, the Lord is intensely interested in our choices and will guide us to things we didn't even know were possible.[10]

As our search for God's will expands from a few personal choices to all of life, what we seek to understand becomes more focused. We are looking to understand God's character— what Peter called the knowledge of him who called us to his own glory and excellence. God made and redeemed us so that we would make our decisions and do all things as Christ would if he faced the same situations. Thus, our Heavenly Father's desire for us is the same as our desire for our children. Of course, we are happy when our children reach their goals of a new car or a good job, but what is that compared to seeing them do justice, love kindness, and walk humbly with their God?[11] Such children have become kingdom builders. Biblical knowledge isn't about finding a shortcut to something that seems attractive. It's about learning the character of Christ that God intends to be mine.

It is misguided, therefore, to think that the law of God is irrelevant for Christians because Christ has saved us from the divine judgment we deserve. Yes, we are entirely free from the law's curse; praise God! But how could we be free from all the goodness and wisdom God loves? Why would we want to be?

---

[9] 1 Corinthians 2:9-16.
[10] 2 Chronicles 16:9.
[11] Micah 6:8.

The place of biblical knowledge in Peter's Principles

With biblical knowledge, we extend Peter's list of qualities another step. As saving grace overflows, it generates the desire for virtue, the deep aspiration to be like Jesus. Scripture gives us knowledge of what that entails so we can seek virtue in our current situation. Forgiveness of wrongs done to me? Patience? Simple goodwill? Management of strong impulses? Wise caution? Contentment? Labor for someone's welfare? Accomplishing a task with integrity? Risking rejection to do good? Humble perseverance no matter what? Implementing godly ways to govern or do business? There are a great many applications of Christ's character and love. What would Jesus think, understand, feel, and want in my current position? Not if I were Jesus, who wore sandals, walked in a Jewish/Roman world, and came to die for the sins of mankind, but rather if the Holy Spirit cultivated Christ's character and love in me so I could build God's kingdom right now in Jesus' name.

Knowledge plays a crucial role in discipleship but only when properly related to the surrounding qualities in Peter's list. Knowledge does no good and does not make us good by itself. As the Apostle Paul said, "knowledge puffs up, but love builds up."[12] When biblical knowledge is isolated, it results in one of two things.

The first relates to Peter's previous steps. If Bible instruction is not the overflow of aspiration, it will be half-heartedly received and poorly absorbed. Aspiration for Christ's virtue drives us to the Bible because we need answers to pursue the high calling of following Christ. Without aspiration, however, good sermons will be boring, group Bible study won't get beyond socializing, and personal Bible study will be erratic, unfocussed, or non-existent.

The second result of isolated Bible knowledge relates to the steps going forward. If Bible knowledge is not put to use by self-control, it can become counterproductive. Not acting upon

---

[12] 1 Corinthians 8:1.

the truth we learn tends to desensitize the conscience. We get used to the illusion that knowledge alone makes us more godly. We can reach the point where we regularly discuss spiritual matters and praise good teaching without the slightest intent to change anything we think, feel, or do. Repeatedly doing this blinds us to sins we have shielded from the truth for so long that we are no longer aware of them. We tolerate the presence of grudges, secret habits, hateful prejudices, and many other sins as familiar furniture in our souls. Were any of these sins the subject of a sermon, we would congratulate ourselves on our superior knowledge about such things while doing nothing about what we've heard.

There is a commonly told Navaho story of the conscience as a triangle in the heart. When the conscience is active, the triangle rotates, and the sharp points alert us that something is wrong. But if we harden our hearts, the triangle's points eventually wear off, leaving a smooth edge that no longer raises the alarm. So each time we praise "great teaching" yet do nothing in response to follow Jesus more faithfully, the more our inner conscience is worn down.

Jesus said, "If you know these things, blessed are you if you do them."[13] There is no godliness in unused truth. The more knowledge we learn without putting it into practice, the more spiritually calcified we become.

Knowledge in the pursuit of Christ's mission

Biblical knowledge is crucial to Christ's mission. Without it, we can do much construction but build little that lasts because we have used the wrong blueprint or building materials.

> According to the grace of God given to me, like a skilled master builder I laid a foundation, and someone else is building upon it. Let each one take care of how he builds upon it. For no one can lay a foundation other than that

---

[13] John 13:17.

which is laid, which is Jesus Christ. Now if anyone builds on the foundation with gold, silver, precious stones, wood, hay, straw—each one's work will become manifest, for the Day will disclose it, because it will be revealed by fire, and the fire will test what sort of work each one has done. If the work that anyone has built on the foundation survives, he will receive a reward. If anyone's work is burned up, he will suffer loss, though he himself will be saved, but only as through fire. (1 Corinthians 3:10-15)

Goals, principles, values, and priorities that only reflect those of our society are shoddy building materials for God's kingdom. They may build our kingdom but not his. Extending the realm where God rules requires accurate knowledge of the character, love, and mission of Jesus Christ.

§

As we gain biblical knowledge, the next step in discipleship is obvious. We must *use* the knowledge of God's will that aspiration has moved us to discover.

Discussion Questions for Chapter 7

1. Have you ever had to do or assemble something without adequate instructions?
2. What are some consequences of passionately pursuing God without knowing what God has said about himself?
3. How have Christians been freed from God's law?
   a) How is it still useful for Christians today?
4. Discuss the meaning of Deuteronomy 29:29: "The secret things belong to the LORD our God, but the things that are revealed belong to us and to our children forever, that we may do all the words of this law."
   a) How does this relate to the question of whether God is our Sherpa or Shepherd?
5. Why is biblical knowledge less helpful when detached from its place in Peter's ordered list of elements?

Chapter 8: Self-Control

For this very reason, make every effort to supplement your faith with virtue, and virtue with knowledge, **and knowledge with self-control**, and self-control with steadfastness, and steadfastness with godliness, and godliness with brotherly affection, and brotherly affection with love. (2 Peter 1:5-7)

One morning Peter awoke early to find that Jesus was not in the house. People began to cluster outside, so Peter gathered a few others to find him. He came across Jesus praying as dawn broke, looking out over the shoreline of the Sea of Galilee.

They found him and said to him, "Everyone is looking for you." And he said to them, "Let us go on to the next towns, that I may preach there also, for that is why I came out."
And he went throughout all Galilee, preaching in their synagogues and casting out demons. (Mark 1:37-39)

§

Discipleship uses rich metaphors to fuel our aspirations and translate them into something actionable. For a disciple, the principle metaphor is "following Jesus." The idea of following Jesus has been a metaphor since Jesus ascended. It continues to be helpful because Jesus sent his Spirit to come alongside us as we walk through life.

In the beginning, though, following Jesus wasn't a metaphor. To follow Jesus meant to physically leave where you were and go with him wherever he went. Jesus did not say, "I'm going on to the next towns, that I may preach there also." Instead, he said, "Let *us* go on to the next towns ...." For Peter, following Jesus meant packing an overnight bag. Those first few forays were probably short and close by, wending back to Capernaum and the shelter of Peter's home. Then they involved camping out or staying with receptive folk in the towns they visited. That turned into longer stretches away, traveling as far as Jerusalem to the south and Mount Hermon to the north. Peter's journey with Christ would eventually take him from Jerusalem to Rome.

But leaving home had not been part of the deal when Peter first met Jesus or when Jesus followed Peter and the others back to Capernaum and lodged at Peter's house. That's why this early morning search for Jesus was critical in Peter's life. Up to that point, following Jesus had meant opening up his life to the Master. Jesus had come into his home, joined his family, and taught from his house in the community Peter had known from childhood. A passage from the Book of Revelation comes to mind in which Jesus asks a church to open its door to him so that he might come in and fellowship with them.[1] Peter had done that; he had opened to Jesus the door of his home and heart.

But finding Jesus that morning marked a change. Jesus spoke about what was important to *him*, the very reason he was born. Jesus opened the door of his heart to Peter and asked his disciple to come in. This was the first time Peter chose to obey Jesus by doing something he had never done before, only because Jesus asked him to.

To find us, the Son of God trailed our sin down to this broken world, through the cross, to where we live. He followed and found us to give what Peter calls "an inheritance

---

[1] Revelation 3:20.

that is imperishable, undefiled, and unfading, kept in heaven for you."[2] Jesus then asks us to follow him.

Putting substance to the metaphor: following Jesus means doing what he asks. It means obeying him.

The missing word in discipleship

In the modern American church, life-changing obedience is not featured in discipleship. To demonstrate, please humor me by reading through this familiar quote:

> All authority in heaven and on earth has been given to me. Go therefore and make disciples of all nations, baptizing them in the name of the Father and of the Son and of the Holy Spirit, teaching them all that I have commanded you. And behold, I am with you always, to the end of the age. (Matthew 28:18-20)

It is astounding and concerning how many of us believe the above quote is the Great Commission. I confess that I deliberately misquoted the Bible. The Great Commission actually reads, "teaching them *to observe* [obey] all that I have commanded." I fear that many Christians overlook this element of making disciples. Perhaps we think of obedience as being included in teaching.

But we do not typically teach to achieve obedience. I understood this in a discussion with my daughter, Renee, after decades of pastoral ministry. In her corporate job, she provides materials for computer-assisted learning. She pointed out that her company was not interested in what she could academically teach employees and customers; they were interested in what she could help them learn to *do*. I immediately realized that by comparison, the Church teaches only for understanding, not for actual lifestyle change.

The method of Christian training we are accustomed to is almost entirely academic. We teach for understanding, which is how America academically educates from grade school through college. We read, discuss, listen to lectures, and take

---

[2] 1 Peter 1:4.

tests to demonstrate our intellectual understanding. In church, we learn a great deal of truth. Such instruction is, of course, essential. If I joined a wagon train going West to California, I would want to know as much as possible about what to expect, so I could prepare and make plans. But learning everything there is to know about the journey West would not get me one mile closer to California. The trip would require me to get on my wagon and start moving. If Christ commissions the Church to make disciples by teaching them to obey, then discipleship should train me to make the lifestyle changes needed to follow Jesus.

Think of discipleship in light of Jesus' famous claim:

> I am the way, and the truth, and the life. No one comes to the Father except through me. (John 14:6)

Jesus is the truth, so learning truth from him and about him is crucial. Jesus is the life, so we need faith in him for eternal life in God's fellowship. But what about Jesus as the way? The way is, literally, the road. It is my path through life—how I choose to live or, as we say it today, my lifestyle. The Church teaches how to study the Bible for truth and rest in faith for eternal life. It must also train believers to live like Jesus.

Yet, almost all Christian education is exclusively academic. We teach *about* things. We teach about God and Christ and sin and salvation. We teach the Bible's message, the Bible's stories, the Bible's characters, the Bible's books, the Bible's language, and the Bible's history. It's excellent, and it's necessary, but virtually all academic. That's true from the earliest Sunday School to thousands of preached sermons and even seminary courses. This is all very good; we must be educated in the Bible and have a Christian worldview. Making disciples requires an academic component. The problem is that discipleship also requires hands-on practice to live differently.

"But doesn't good teaching include application?" Yes. But we teach *about* application. We do not expect anyone to demonstrate that they have actually applied anything.

Academic instruction is essential. Learning and relating facts that lead to personal conclusions is necessary for growth. But when this is all that discipleship prepares us for, Christians unconsciously develop the illusion that we have learned something when we have only learned about it. Or even worse, we have learned something because we have heard someone talk about it, whether or not we can even remember what they said.

This is not the model of discipleship Jesus used. Discipleship meant apprenticeship, and how many apprenticeships are only academic? Imagine using such a model to train plumbers or airline pilots. What kind of plumbers and pilots would we have if they never learned to do anything more, differently, or better than before they were trained?

"But how can you train Christians to live differently? All we can do is present the truth and hope people pick it up." Is this what we say when teaching customer service, medicine, or any practical subject? "Just read this material and pass a test showing you read it. Demonstrating that you can do the job is not part of the training." Is that the sort of lawyer or electrician you want to hire? Does getting a driver's license only require describing how a person should drive?

"But the Church can't make people do things." Of course, it can't. Neither would Jesus force anyone to follow him. But disciples are people who have already committed themselves to follow. Jesus trained his disciples to feel, think, and act differently. Christ not only explained to them the nature of love in words but also personally illustrated love by example. He exposed the disciples to real people around them who were unloving. He had the disciples assist him as he loved others and corrected his disciples personally and pointedly when they failed to love. He sent his disciples to practice what he taught and report how it went. Following Jesus involves more than understanding; it involves obedience.

To keep the term "Christian education" a synonym for discipleship, we must make practice part of the curriculum. There are contexts where training like this is done, as in internships for some ordained positions. But discipleship is meant for all believers. How many of us have had anything like an internship in being a Christian? Discipleship involves learning how to live in God's kingdom. Since his kingdom is different from the culture we know, living in it consists of thinking, feeling, and doing things *differently*. It requires change. It requires obedience to Christ.

One reason we shy away from practicing obedience is that it requires supervision. An apprentice needs a master or trainer, but whom would we trust to reshape who we are? That is an appropriate concern. I only know of one such person I would trust: Jesus Christ. Fortunately, he is available for the job through the active presence of the Holy Spirit. People we call disciple-makers are not our Head Coach. They are more like assistant player-coaches. The Apostle Paul expressed that when he said, "Be imitators of me, as I am of Christ."[3] The Church is called to provide disciple-makers who teach and provide active examples of obedience, but our obedience is always to Christ alone.[4] Coaches help us discern real from imagined progress, but we are not accountable to them any more than we wish to be. In fact, a single coach is not required. Any church will have members who stand out in different aspects of character and love. Each could help us become more like Christ if we imitated them in a particular way. Small groups of like-minded disciples can provide powerful mutual encouragement as long as a more experienced guide is available to help them stay on the right path.[5] A church must only provide the core means of grace and coordinate all this. That is what pastors are for.[6]

Obedience and self-control

Obedience is most often described by that single word. But Peter describes obedience with two sequentially related

---

[3] 1 Corinthians 11:1.
[4] Matthew 23:8-12.
[5] Hebrews 10:24-25; 1 Corinthians 14:26-29.
[6] Ephesians 4:11-13.

words: self-control and steadfastness. Self-control describes our initial obedience in a given area. Steadfastness then continues that same obedience through trial until it becomes our new lifestyle. We will study these two steps separately, self-control in this chapter and steadfastness in the next.

Obedience must begin somewhere. In every aspect of God's will, before I can become steadfast in following Christ, there must be a first time that I change what I have been doing and choose to obey God by doing it differently. I will discover thousands of things about my new identity that require change, some big and some small. I can't deal with them all in this life, and I can't handle many at once. But each one I address will require an initial period of self-control because it involves a change of habit—one I am making only because Jesus asks me to.

The Greek word Peter uses for self-control originally described physical or intellectual power but, over time, came to focus on control over one's self and, in particular, over one's physical desires. It is here that self-control begins. God built physical desires into us and designed them to bring joy. However, since fallen mankind is predisposed to ignore the divine design still echoing in our consciences, we typically mishandle our desires and satisfy them inappropriately. That often means bending our conscience around how we intend to indulge ourselves.

When Christian hearts overflow with gospel grace, they want to become like Jesus and start to learn from the Bible what that means. The first serious challenges involve physical desires like hunger, sex, and comfort. We face them first because they are hard-wired, universal impulses that manifest themselves whether or not we want them to. They represent some of the fundamental forms of human pleasure. All such hard-wired pleasures are gifts of God to humanity. They reflect a Creator who thinks pleasure is a great idea and wants it to be part of our lives.

> You will make known to me the way of life;
> In Your presence is fullness of joy;

In Your right hand there are pleasures forever. (Psalm 16:11)

God ... richly supplies us with all things to enjoy. (1 Timothy 6:17)

When the Apostle Paul argued against forced abstinence from certain foods or sexual intimacy in marriage, he reasoned,

For everything created by God is good, and nothing is to be rejected if it is received with gratitude; for it is sanctified by means of the word of God and prayer. (1 Timothy 4:4-5)

However, while physical pleasures are blessings from God, they are, in themselves, morally neutral. It is how we choose to satisfy them in a given situation that creates a moral choice. Do we choose satisfaction according to God's design or in another way? For example, eating a whole sandwich is a blessing. But if only one has a sandwich and two are hungry, the right thing to do may be for both to share the hunger and the pleasure of eating—a moral choice.

Sexual intimacy is a blessing. Someone who self-identifies in terms of cosmic chance may satisfy that desire with anyone available whom they find desirable. However, someone who self-identifies as a follower of Jesus will trust in God's design of the family and seek to satisfy the same desire according to monogamous, heterosexual marriage—a moral choice.[7]

Comfort is a great blessing. But history is full of inspiring examples, great drama, and enduring legends involving a voluntary acceptance of pain for the sake of another's good—moral choices.

---

[7] Marriage is a major and holy Bible theme because it portrays the intended relationship between God and his people. It runs throughout the Scriptures from creation to the exodus, to the exile, to Jesus and his work, to apostolic teaching, all the way to Jesus at his return to take his Bride, the Church.

These examples illustrate the nature and necessity of self-control. It's easy to convince ourselves that since pleasure is God's blessing, we can pursue it however we like. While that is often true (God has not instructed us to prefer peas over corn, for example), where God has specified a specific design for human life, we should enjoy pleasure as God directs.

Over time, discipleship expands self-control into all of life. It may begin with managing our physical desires differently but quickly grows to include any desire—not only the built-in physical ones but all the others we cultivate or have had impressed upon us by society: our taste in entertainment, the vocabulary we use, loyalty to our country or political party, spending habits—all the values and preferences that determine how we live day by day. Each involves overlapping desires that require self-control to manage according to God's revealed will. Where our habits have strayed from God's design, disciples want to consciously guide their thoughts, direct their speech, and manage their behavior back toward God's likeness in Christ.

The nature of obedience

Self-control becomes a mockery of obedience when it involves external behavior only. That is how Pharisees are made. Pharisees exercised considerable willpower to obey rules, but Jesus called them hypocrites because their actions were not internally motivated by God's character and love. Starting from self-control and working backward down Peter's steps, Pharisees:

- did not correctly understand the Scriptures.[8]
- aspired to impress people rather than manifest God's virtues.[9]
- did not have saving faith.[10]

---

[8] Mark 12:24; Matthew 6:5.
[9] Matthew 23:23-28.
[10] Matthew 21:33-44; John 8:21-24 (cf. vs. 3 to identify his hearers).

Working forward up Peter's steps, their brand of self-control

- did not enable them to love God.[11]
- did not enable them to love fellow believers (Jews).[12]
- did not enable them to love everyone.[13]

Christian discipleship teaches a better kind of obedience than that practiced by Pharisees because it is more than outward duty from an uninvolved heart.[14] True obedience trusts that God knows what is best, desires the best for me, has the right to determine how I should live, and in Christ, shows me what that is. Obedience willingly wraps my will around God's so that I want what he wants more than I want anything else. Obedience always has an element of joy even when it is painful because we are confident its outcome will contribute to God's glory and my good. The extreme example is the obedience of Jesus: "who for the joy that was set before him endured the cross."[15]

Obedience is the outcome of repentance, another concept profoundly misunderstood as merely a behavior change. The word *repent* means "to change one's mind" about something. Biblical repentance requires the confidence and gratitude of saving faith, the powerful aspiration to become like Christ, and a balanced grasp of God's will. When I have thus changed my understanding and emotions, I can honestly and willingly change my actions. Like uprooting tree stumps in a field, repentance and obedience are never easy because change is not easy. But I can sing while I work with the Holy Spirit, who has given me the vision of a new homestead.

---

[11] Mark 7:6.

[12] Luke 11:46.

[13] In debate, Jesus interpreted the Old Testament "love your neighbor" as love for anyone. Luke 10:25-37.

[14] Matthew 5:17-20.

[15] Hebrews 12:2.

Given the ruin of my sin and the glory of Christ, I want to change in many ways. Unfortunately, in my short life span here, I can only address a limited number. Therefore, each occasion of self-control initiating a heartfelt and intelligent change in my lifestyle should be celebrated and cherished. Each milestone tells me that I am closer to discovering who I am in Christ.

My story

The first act of obedience to Christ that I remember occurred in 1970. I was in Michigan at a two-week InterVarsity summer camp for college students studying the Lordship of Christ. I'm still enjoying fruit from those two weeks all these many years later. One of our workshops was about leading evangelistic Bible studies in our dorm. I liked letting the Bible speak for itself and thought I might attend one. The IV staff worker teaching the workshop said she asked the Lord to raise 30 of us to start such a study in the coming Fall.

Attending a study was one thing, but leading one? In my dorm? I already stood out because of a housing assignment error. I was supposed to be assigned to Cambridge A, the honors dorm, but instead found myself in Cambridge B, the basketball dorm. I am not a basketball player. Because of my longish hair and cross around my neck, the basketball players good-naturedly called me a Jesus Freak. I got along well with everyone—but holding a Bible study in my hall? I didn't want to do that.

But as the two-week camp drew to a close, I realized I *did* want to do that. It felt strange and risky, but I sensed it was something Jesus wanted me to do. So for that reason alone, I decided to do it. Two students would profess faith through that study, and one became my college roommate.

I chose this example to illustrate that self-control is not only about changing bad habits. That Bible study was an instance of self-control because it was the first time I did something I had never done before just because I believed that Jesus wanted me to do it. It expanded my life tremendously. It showed me that self-control is an essentially positive experience, even when challenging.

Oh yes, I should mention that as I was on the final bus leaving for home, I remembered that I hadn't told the staff worker I planned to lead a study. So I jumped off and found her sitting alone with her head bowed in one of the large empty conference rooms. I apologized for interrupting but told her of my plans. She lifted her head with a brilliant smile, saying, "You are number 30."

The place of self-control in Peter's Principles

We are constantly tempted to isolate the steps which Peter connects. In isolation, self-control sounds similar to any number of worldly self-help programs. But taken as a whole, Peter's sequence of qualities describes what it means to abide in Christ through the Holy Spirit. It always begins by reconnecting with faith in God's unchangeable love for me in Christ. Aspiration stands on this, yearning to discover my new self in Christ's virtue. Biblical truth reveals the person God intended me to be. I walk in step with the Spirit as aspiration and knowledge combine to initiate a different thought, feeling, or action. We abide in Christ when it all engages at once, accomplishing change that formerly seemed impossible.

In other words, obedience is a response to God's grace motivated in the heart and understood by the mind. I have seen in movies secure locks used to release immense power. They require two keys turned at precisely the same time. While resting in gospel grace, Christ-like obedience only engages when aspiration and knowledge are active *simultaneously*. When that happens, we release the power to change.

At this point, we can appreciate that previous steps in Peter's Principles are not projects we check off when completed and then move on. When you climb a staircase, you cannot allow the lower section to be removed as you go. You need it to support you where you are and enable you to climb higher. When we put Peter's previous steps into storage, we can't use them to step up to the obedience that builds God's kingdom. The best we can hope for is an unhappy duty that seems to obey on the outside while masking an inner unwillingness or self-pity. That does not describe the obedience of Jesus. His Sermon on the Mount repeatedly emphasized that true obedience stems from what we want and understand on the inside.[16]

The Apostle Paul followed that logic further when he said: "Do not be overcome by evil, but overcome evil with good."[17] Self-control is only secondarily a matter of self-denial. Primarily, self-control is an intelligent and passionate determination to make space for something better. This leads to the surprising realization that all self-control born of Peter's Principles is, on balance, a positive experience. We have old habits of body and mind, built-in physical desires, emotions, and opinions, which have hardened over time to form barriers to God's design. But if we pursue Peter's Principles, we develop much more than a sense of obligation. A sense of obligation is merely an awareness of how we *ought* to change. Self-control born of Peter's Principles expresses a redeemed sense of how we *want* to change.

Let me say that another way. Obedience won't happen until I want it to happen. Obedience *can't* happen until I want it to happen because obedience involves my heart and mind as well as my behavior. When an old way of living blocks my journey with Jesus, exercising willpower alone can't get me over it; if it could, I would have overcome it before now. I can't overcome it either because I don't yet sufficiently want to or don't yet understand God's will.

When I am stopped by a challenge to my spiritual growth —a wall I can't get over—I imagine building a small two-tread staircase that rests securely on God's unshakable love in Christ. The first tread is a desire to discover the new me in Jesus' virtue. The second tread is biblical insight about what that new me looks like. This small staircase gets me high enough to exercise willpower and make it over the barrier. I

---

[16] Matthew 5:21-6:4 illustrates this time and again.
[17] Romans 12:21.

need to consciously bring out this small staircase of aspiration and insight each day for a while. If I neglect to do so, the barrier will again stop me. But if I use it consistently, it becomes steadfast (next chapter), permanently built-in to access a new path for my life.

Self-control in the pursuit of Christ's mission

Christ's mission is to grow God's kingdom in and through us, and growth requires change. If we cannot generate the self-control for that change, kingdom growth gets stuck. I daresay every church and every Christian always faces resistance to some needed change, and kingdom expansion within us or through is put on hold while we work it out.

When I realize I'm stuck and decide to do something about it, I should look back to the previous step to see if I have misunderstood the Bible. Then, looking further back, I need to check whether my aspiration to follow Christ is fresh or stale. I may even need to go all the way back to see if my soul is motivated by God's overwhelming grace. Successful self-control requires that I first go back and address any obstructions upstream. Peter's steps always have to work together.

But if the earlier steps give me enough stability and height, the barrier is no longer too difficult. Faith-based motivation and biblical understanding have lifted me so that obedience has become manageable. I need not hesitate further. I can step out and boldly go where I, at least, have never gone before.

There is a scene in the movie version of *The Fellowship of the Ring* when Frodo and Sam leave the small Shire, the only home they have known, for a trek that will take them on a fantastic adventure. They travel some distance and reach the end of a particular field. Frodo continues, but Sam stops. After a moment, Sam says, "This is it. If I take one more step, it will be the farthest away from home I've ever been." I imagine everyone who has viewed that scene understands Sam's feelings. It's a natural hesitation. But Sam had already made up his mind and packed his things. He was determined to follow Frodo. He was ready. He only needed to go ahead and take the next step, and that's what he did—adequate preparation and then obedience—that is how self-control works.

We will see in the next chapter that steadfastness is about turning initial obedience into a lifestyle. Self-control is about that initial obedience, taking the kingdom of God further within me and into the world by doing something I've never done before because Jesus asks me to. I might start something, stop something, or do something differently. What I do might be private or public, impressively large or mundanely small. But I must do it *once*. I need not worry about long-term life changes but exercise self-control to do something the first few times. I need to show the Lord and show myself that, despite my hesitation, I've already made up my mind, packed my things, and am determined to follow Jesus. I am ready. Just as so many have watched Sam take his next step, the Lord watches each of his children whenever we do the same.

> For the eyes of the LORD move to and fro throughout the earth that He may strongly support those whose heart is completely His. (2 Chronicles 16:9, NASV)

God will support me with his almighty power whenever I am confident in his love, long to follow Jesus, know what that means, and obey him in a new way for the first time. I may feel weak because it is new to me, but it is in such weakness that God delights to manifest his strength.[18] He is like a parent watching children take their first steps. Children have their parents' complete attention in such moments; should they fall, they will be caught by loving and happy arms.

§

Of course, obedience is more than an initial venture of self-control. It is more than a beginning. So we naturally move to

---

[18] 2 Corinthians 12:9.

the next step in Peter's Principles, the second element of obedience.

Discussion Questions for Chapter 8

1. Share a memorable experience from your younger years about doing something for the first time.
2. Did you notice in the chapter when the Great Commission was misquoted?
   a) Discuss the difference between teaching what Jesus commanded and teaching to obey what Jesus commanded.
   b) Apply this comparison to any practical apprenticeship.
3. Discuss how the way we indulge our natural appetites relates to our sense of identity.
4. Besides directing our natural appetites, what else in us needs to change if we are to become like Jesus?
5. How could it be that "all self-control born of Peter's Principles is, on balance, a positive experience"?
   a) How does it feel to know that the Lord is happily watching as you obey Christ in a new way for the first time?

Chapter 9: Steadfastness

> For this very reason, make every effort to supplement your faith with virtue, and virtue with knowledge, and knowledge with self-control, **and self-control with steadfastness**, and steadfastness with godliness, and godliness with brotherly affection, and brotherly affection with love. (2 Peter 1:5-7)

Public teaching and private instruction were only a part of Peter's discipleship. Most of his time was spent helping Jesus address every kind of need imaginable while dealing with increasing conflict with religious leaders. Peter learned by observing Jesus' motives, reactions, and words while dining with people from all walks of life. He saw Jesus up close while traveling over too many days and nights to keep track of. Peter watched Jesus practice what he preached.

For Jesus, obedience to God was a way of life. Perhaps that is why, before the word "church" was used to describe Jesus' followers, they were called "The Way."[1] Christ had called Peter to a faith that brought the kingdom of God to earth. For over three years, Jesus modeled that way of life in a wider variety of situations than most people ever find themselves. Jesus' goal, however, was that his disciples would do more than watch and listen. He wanted them to love God and others as

---

[1] Acts 9:2; 19:9,23; 22:4,14,22; 25:3.

he did. This required more than individual instances of obedience. They would have to embrace new lives that thought and felt as he did, saw reality in terms of God's kingdom, and embraced his mission as their own.[2]

Change on that level is not easy. I'm sure every disciple had his own path of change, but the New Testament gives us a detailed example of only one. The matter of Peter's transformation is taken up immediately after his glorious confession of Christ.

> And he asked them, "But who do you say that I am?" Peter answered him, "You are the Christ." And he strictly charged them to tell no one about him.
>
> And [Jesus] began to teach them that the Son of Man must suffer many things and be rejected by the elders and the chief priests and the scribes and be killed, and after three days rise again. And he said this plainly. And Peter took him aside and began to rebuke him. But turning and seeing his disciples, he rebuked Peter and said, "Get behind me, Satan! For you are not setting your mind on the things of God, but on the things of man." (Mark 8:29-33)

As is true with every believer, Peter was called by grace and not because of what he deserved or earned. Peter was not the Rock because he was so strong and stable. He was the Rock because God the Father revealed Jesus' identity to him when it was time for the kingdom to grow. Peter's journey would involve learning to rely on God's strength instead of his own.

This was something all the disciples had to learn. It was intimately related to leadership and authority. Leaders in the world believe that their position revolves around them and depends on their strengths. Jesus wanted them to see things differently.

---

[2] John 17:6-18; 20:21-22.

> You know that those who are considered rulers of the
> Gentiles lord it over them, and their great ones exercise
> authority over them. But it shall not be so among you. But
> whoever would be great among you must be your servant,
> and whoever would be first among you must be slave of all.
> For even the Son of Man came not to be served but to
> serve, and to give his life as a ransom for many."
> (Mark 10:42-45)

Jesus taught and exemplified a leadership that revolved around God and the people God calls. And it depends on a kind of weakness instead of strength.

This made no sense to Peter and even led to a confrontation during the Last Supper when Jesus illustrated his leadership by washing the disciples' feet. The crisis came in Gethsemane. Peter responded with raw courage when the Temple guards arrived to make their arrest. Earlier, at the Passover table, Peter declared that even if all others fled, he would use all his strength to fight for Jesus.[3] But Jesus' willingness to be arrested made it apparent that Peter's strength was not critical in the kingdom of God. This led a confused and despondent Peter to deny Christ later that night.

Only after the cross and resurrection did Peter begin to understand. Jesus never intended to save himself through a demonstration of power. Jesus was determined to save us, and he did it through weakness. Jesus voluntarily allowed himself to be crucified to maintain God's righteousness as he poured out love to sinners. Jesus showed that God's power is best revealed through human weakness and sacrifice. This was not easy for Peter to accept. It contradicted his assumptions and left him stunned while Jesus died alone. Peter lacked the courage to serve in weakness so that God's power and love could shine. Perhaps he wasn't cut out to be a disciple after all.

The risen Christ said he would meet the eleven remaining disciples in Galilee.[4] As they waited for their Master, Peter had

---

[3] Mark 14:26-31.

[4] John 21:1-19.

time for some fishing. It was something he knew, something he was good at. But it turned into another one of those rare all-nighters when he caught nothing. As dawn broke, a voice from shore asked if he had caught anything. He hadn't. "Cast the net on the right side of the boat, and you will find some." Sure enough, there were more fish than the boat could hold.

It all came back to Peter—his first lesson when he saw the needs of others through the Master's eyes and then experienced Jesus bringing in a boatload of fish through his hands after an all-night failure. Jesus hadn't chosen Peter for his strengths! Peter was chosen to reveal God's love as the Lord manifested divine power through him. Peter left his friends to deal with the fish and quickly swam to shore.

After breakfast (fish, of course), Jesus had one more private conversation with the man called Simon when they first met. He called Peter by his old name, asking whether Simon loved him enough to care for his Church. He kept repeating the question until the exasperated fisherman said Jesus must know the answer because the Son of God could see who he really was. That was the point Jesus was making: he could see who Simon *really* was. The man who had studied Jesus' character and love was discovering his own true identity. Yes, *Peter* would care for Christ's Church and do it as Christ would because Jesus' Spirit lived in and through him, as God originally intended. Jesus then confirmed that the man he had discipled would indeed have the courage to manifest God's love in weakness, even unto death. And finally, for one last time, he said to his friend, "Follow me."

Not long after Jesus' ascension, Peter got his first opportunity to demonstrate the power of God's love. The Feast of Pentecost drew thousands of Jews from many nations to celebrate in Jerusalem. Jesus said that the worldwide expansion of God's kingdom would start there—but how? The disciples had no plan and no finances. So Peter led them to do what they could. They showed up, and they prayed.

If Peter had tried to instigate some grand plan in his strength, we wouldn't be talking about Pentecost today. Instead, God manifested his power through an astounding universal language! Suddenly, the crowd needed someone to explain to them what message was so important that people worldwide needed to hear it. Peter stood up and once again saw the crowd through Jesus' eyes. He told them what Jesus had told him, adding the resurrection he and the others had witnessed. Peter watched a miracle happen through him but not by his power. Three thousand people found God's goodness and love in Jesus and began a new life. That sermon was Peter's first act of self-control to let God powerfully demonstrate his love quite apart from Peter's strength.

The Book Acts shows Peter becoming steadfast in his ministry by practicing that initial Pentecost obedience through many trials and challenges. He is always the weakest one in the room, but when the dust clears, it's God's goodness and love that is remembered. He developed the steadfast lifestyle of serving others in weakness as Jesus did, expecting God to manifest his power and love. He was never disappointed. We'll see more examples in the chapters ahead.

Peter ultimately discovered the man whom, at first, only Jesus saw. He had once relied on his strength to write his own story. Now, he relied on God's strength to tell Jesus' story. Perhaps the most telling comment about the "new" Peter came from the ruling authorities as they remarked how he reminded them of someone:

> Now when they saw the boldness of Peter and John, and perceived that they were uneducated, common men, they were astonished. And they recognized that they had been with Jesus. (Acts 4:13)

§

Discovering our true identity in Christ is a process. Peter laid out what that process involves for any believer:

- Cultivate our gratitude and enthusiasm over gospel grace into a passion for following Jesus, becoming like him, and working his mission alongside him.

- Channel that passion into the expectant study of the Scriptures.
- Courageously experiment with new ways of living that embody Scriptural truth.

Once we exercise self-control to obey in a new way, we will want to evaluate what we did and its outcome. We may wish to consult mature Christians to help us decide if our new obedience was on target or should be adjusted to hit closer to the bullseye of God's will.

When we are satisfied that our new obedience is on target, there is one more step in developing Jesus' character. This last step turns the novelty of new obedience into a modified lifestyle. This is where true transformation happens. To self-control, we must add steadfastness.

The Greek word translated as "steadfastness" in the New Testament comes from the root of "be patient, persevere, and endure." However, the English ideas of patience and endurance can be understood in several ways. One is the idea of bearing with difficulty until a trial is past, that is, getting through a rough patch. We've all had such challenges. (I think of the three root canals, two surgeries, and the implant I have endured because of one failed tooth!) Enduring pain until it is over is part of steadfastness, but that understanding misses the key biblical idea. Look at how New Testament authors used this Greek word. I'll highlight with italics the English translation of the same word Peter uses, but please focus on what each verse describes.

As for that in the good soil, they are those who, hearing the word, hold it fast in an honest and good heart, and bear fruit with *patience*. (Luke 8:15)

To those who by *patience* in well-doing seek for glory and honor and immortality, he will give eternal life. (Romans 2:7)

For you have need of *endurance*, so that when you have done the will of God you may receive what is promised. (Hebrews 10:36)

I know your works, love, faith, service, and patient *endurance*, and that your latter works exceed the first. (Revelation 2:19)

Endurance with a purpose

While steadfastness does involve bearing with challenges over the long haul, it is not a passive gritting of teeth to get past suffering. The Scriptures quoted above show that in the New Testament, the word is best captured by the English word *persevere*. Steadfastness refers to persistence in doing something or being something, even through a difficult patch. It is not about just getting past the challenge but maintaining an action or attitude through the challenge. In the above scriptural examples, steadfastness means holding fast to the Word, well-doing that seeks glory and honor, and doing the will of God in works of love, faith, and service—actively persisting in those things, even through pain, distraction, or resistance. Steadfastness is not passive; it is active faithfulness despite trial and distress.

A simple illustration may help. Imagine a scene in a Western where a stagecoach driver pushes the horses for all they are worth because one of the passengers is ill or wounded. They've got to get to the nearest doctor as quickly as possible to save that life. Other passengers comfort and encourage the wounded one, urging him to hang on until they reach help. The injured person does need to hang on, but that is not the quality Peter is talking about. The steadfastness Peter is talking about is better illustrated by the stagecoach driver (and the horses!), who must battle fatigue to get to town in time. No matter what it costs them, they must press on to do what must be done.

Steadfastness is purposeful. It involves endurance but also implies a goal. Steadfastness is about being and doing what you need to be and do despite pain or other hindrance. Christians realize that God defines what we must pursue. It's not about sticking to your dreams no matter what but instead remaining faithful to Christ no matter what. In terms of Peter's Principles, steadfastness is maintaining a new act of Christ-like obedience regardless of how hard it seems, and no matter how many times you stumble, until it becomes your new lifestyle— in other words, until it becomes you.

At that point, your character has changed in that one area. Note that it has not changed by forcing unwanted behavior. Instead, it has changed from the inside (faith, virtue, knowledge) to the outside (self-control, steadfastness). From your innermost desires to how you live, you are now a little different. You are a little more like Jesus.

Trials and testing

In the Bible, steadfastness is the famous key to character development. As Peter put it,

> ... now for a little while, if necessary, you have been grieved by various trials, so that the tested genuineness of your faith —more precious than gold that perishes though it is tested by fire—may be found to result in praise and glory and honor at the revelation of Jesus Christ. (1 Peter 1:6-7)

The image is how metals like silver, iron, copper, and gold are extracted from raw ore. Extreme heat breaks down existing bonds and frees the metal to collect in pure form. Similarly, the precious new life enjoyed by our reborn heart has pre-existing bonds with old habits of mind, spirit, and body. These bonds together make up the lifestyle modeled off of a world estranged from God and forged by a soul previously dead toward God. Our old lifestyle feels natural, like metal is naturally found in ore that neutralizes the metal's desired qualities. Who would want a gold wedding ring consisting of gold ore? It takes serious heat to break bonds to our old lifestyle and release our valuable and beautiful new life.

Peter's smelting analogy is quite powerful. It helps us realize that the only way to experience and manifest the life of a Christian disciple is through uncomfortable trials. Consider these texts (again, I italicized the underlying Greek word Peter used):

> Not only that, but we rejoice in our sufferings, knowing that suffering produces *endurance*, and *endurance* produces character, and character produces hope (Romans 5:3-4)

> For you know that the testing of your faith produces *steadfastness*. And let *steadfastness* have its full effect, that you may be perfect and complete, lacking in nothing. (James 1:3-4)

One of discipleship's goals is learning how to pursue a "perfect and complete" character. Discipleship trains us to develop the human character of the divine Christ, which we can apply in relationships to extend God's kingdom further.

Character development requires trial and testing, resistance, discomfort, and even pain. Our old bonds to sin are strong. Developing a new character trait involves changing ingrained habits. Steadfastness means continuing the initial self-control that said "No" to something we've always said "Yes" to before or said "Yes" to something we've always said "No" to before. Not doing what we've always done is uncomfortable. It's painful to part with something we have relied on for pleasure, comfort, or security to find those things in something else. Sometimes, it is mildly irritating, like keeping a cell phone for another year to use my money for something more important. Sometimes it is seriously agonizing, like withdrawal from addiction to pain medication.

And the trials we face are not all physical or material. As with Peter, the most deeply ingrained habits involve our values, opinions, and feelings—mental and emotional convictions that seem right because they are so familiar. Change is not easy when we discover they are not right and need adjustment. The change is worthwhile, however, as the wedding ring analogy illustrates. My new life becomes a treasure as it is freed and polished by trials. Neither God nor we can enjoy that treasure until our existing lifestyle bonds are broken.

Peter's take on discipleship is not popular. We prefer an approach that does not require us to make significant changes. After all, it's possible to pray good prayers and insightfully discuss Bible applications without changing our lifestyle in the slightest. That's the kind of apprenticeship we tend to choose, one restricted to reading and discussion without practiced change. The truth, however, is that discipleship is meant to be more like an introduction to weight training or aerobics. Academic instruction helps us approach a new exercise safely, but we grow stronger only when we tolerate some discomfort pushing past resistance to achieve new levels of health and strength.

No rational person chooses pain if there is an alternative. Jesus wanted to avoid the cross if another means of glorifying his Father and saving us was available.[5] He wanted that not because he was weak but because he was sane. Unnecessary suffering is not a good thing. However, since no other way was available, Jesus chose the cross. Since he had been obeying his Father since birth, it was hardly his first act of self-control. Gethsemane was the final expression of his steadfastness.[6]

Since we tend to minimize our trials if we design them ourselves, character development requires trials and tests which are not chosen but come upon us. They provide the opportunity to temper our initial self-control into steadfastness. We change only when we overcome the temptation to abandon obedience to escape the trial. God does not necessarily have to intervene to create such tests; there are plenty that comes upon us naturally in a fallen world. Only a passionate and knowledgeable desire to follow Christ, strong enough to obey through discomfort, will break existing bonds and collect the pure gold of Christ-like character.

This has immense practical significance in understanding the nature of helpful encouragement. A great deal of Christian

---

[5] Matthew 26:36-42.
[6] Hebrews 5:8; cf. verses 7-10.

encouragement for brethren in difficult trials consists of recommending coping mechanisms or pleading to God for escape. Both are appropriate, of course. It is reasonable to seek comfort, peace, patience, and deliverance during severe trials. However, those are not the main things we need. If patience and escape were all we experienced, we would emerge from a trial without any benefit. What we need most is the divine power to remain steadfast in obedience through the challenges to our self-control. Without that, all the pain is wasted, and our lifestyle remains unchanged. It is truly a shame when pain is wasted. If we always reduce the heat of smelting, the workshop will stay comfortably cool, but we'll produce little recognizable gold.

As trials come—and they will, of course—in addition to seeking God's tender mercies, I need to identify aspects of character, love, or mission that are being tested. The encouragement I most need from others is to remain steadfast in those things. Steadfastness through my trial means relying on God's strength as old bonds break and the gold of Christ-like character appears.

Form and function, tools and design

It might be helpful to remember that we are talking broadly about the dynamics of discipleship—the path of spiritual life from faith to love. In practice, steadfastness requires using spiritual disciplines, such as prayer, meditation, and encouragement in small groups. We haven't dealt with these valuable discipleship tools simply because that was not Peter's intent in the text we are studying. Please do not think they are unimportant because I have not included them. Discipleship will always require forms, such as time alone with God, one-to-one mentorships, support groups, and spiritual retreats, each using some combination of spiritual disciplines. Excellent discipleship material exists to explore these tools. Peter does not discuss them here because he is not giving us a program. We are free to construct our own programs.

Peter's steps review God's design for abiding in Christ, the ordered qualities we need to build with the tools of spiritual discipline. We have much excellent teaching on the tools but relatively little on what we must build with them. Peter's structure of qualities implies that no combination of spiritual tools can enable us to jump from faith directly to love. Prayer can't do it. Support groups can't do it. Thinking that they can only leads to frustration and discouragement. What such tools can do, however, is help us to experientially move from one quality to the next anywhere along Peter's ordered steps. This is another insight that's critical to effective discipleship.

My story

Steadfastness is a quality we must always be working on. For me, the last few years have involved learning to use physical pain to make my spiritual focus more down-to-earth. Over the last several years, I have suffered from significant chronic pain brought on by a fall on the ice. After three surgeries and much physical therapy, significant chronic pain remains. I have pleaded to my Lord for help, and he has encouraged my soul, made my pain bearable, and deepened my fellowship with him. But he is also showing me that pain is the environment in which love is beautifully manifested both to me and through me. It is the sad environment in which joy thrives, the restricting environment in which ministry expands. It opens my soul to sense the importance of others by identifying with their suffering. I would say more, but I'm still in the learning stage. What I do know is that while I need God's comfort, peace, and hope, I also need to break old bonds that take comfort for granted and cultivate compassion, sympathy, and empathy for the sake of God's kingdom.

I will mention one other example because it is quite different. It's not about pain but long-term challenges to change from what was once comfortable to something much better. We all grow up learning who we are through parental training, peer groups, school, and thousands of hours of TV and social media, all shaping our decisions and experiences. When we choose something different, just because we believe it to be what God wants us to do, it's a moment of discovery because we uncover a glimpse of the Peter emerging from our Simon. Becoming steadfast in that obedience becomes part of our life's core story.

For me, one track of steadfastness began when I decided to lead that dorm Bible study mentioned in the previous chapter. To understand this, I should mention my early passion for physics. In 1960, when I was ten years old, my parents asked me what I wanted to be when I grew up. I answered, "A theoretical physicist majoring in Quantum Dynamics." I don't think they ever asked me that question again. I read every related book in the library, invented the electrical relay (OK, so I wasn't the first), built a 100,000-volt Tesla coil, and replicated a prototype engine that turned electricity into motion with no moving parts (science fair judges from the Naval Academy were very impressed, even though it had no practical application). At the end of my first year in college (1969), I could speak three different programming languages. I worked with the university cyclotron and the brand-new laser light. I would graduate with honors in Physics, Phi Kappa Phi, and Phi Beta Kappa (unusual for a science major). My Mom was convinced I was on my way to a Nobel Prize (You've got to love a Mom's confidence!). I was dedicated to finding the theory of everything, or at the very least, workable fusion generators that solve the world's energy needs.

I mention all this to emphasize that my interest in science was not casual. It was desperate. I had a deep need to understand reality and my place in it. Science was the only way I knew how to pursue it. I profoundly depended on science to provide meaning.

Then I met the risen Jesus—not like Peter or even Paul, but I met him just the same. I sensed everything had changed from the beginning, but I wasn't sure how. And then, one day, my desire to serve the Lord and my growing knowledge of the Bible teamed up, and I exercised self-control to do something I had never done before just because I believed Jesus wanted me to. I led a Bible study in my dorm despite my anxiety. I had never before done such a thing. So it was a big deal for me.

It was easier to lead a Bible study the second time, meaning it was easier to identify with Christ, talk about him with others, carve out time to prepare, and be gracious to whoever showed up. That experience encouraged me to volunteer in the larger college fellowship and eventually help lead spiritual retreats and seminars. I was then asked to student-lead the local InterVarsity chapter. More and more, people came to me for help to understand God better. I found that not only could the Bible give them answers, but I enjoyed being part of the process.

Shifting from physics to pastoral ministry was neither an obvious nor easy path. The challenge had nothing to do with physics itself but with how I had made it an idol. My values and plans—my entire approach to life—had to change. I mentioned earlier the trauma with my parents. It meant giving up a career they respected for that of a clergyman. (Who wants to be a clergyman?) Some of my friends lost interest in me, for much they admired now seemed to recede into the background. And these challenges were before experiencing actual pastoral ministry.

But each of these challenges highlighted how much I was changing. In my desperate search for meaning, I had always thought of myself as working with computers, theories, and slide rules (look it up). But a time came when I realized that I was finding in Christ the wonder and meaning I had sought in the stars and elementary particles. Then I discovered to my surprise, that I was no longer desperate. Finally, I realized that I wanted to spend my entire life declaring the beauty of God's truth.[7] I'm now retired after 44 years of service. Some parts have been hard, some very hard, but I wouldn't want to have done anything else.

My example does not mean that all Christians will find themselves by leading Bible studies or working professionally in the Church. That was just my story. You have your own story.

---

[7] "Declaring the beauty of God's truth" is my life goal.

I chose this as an example of steadfastness to show that changing how we think and act because we want to follow Jesus is not only about enduring physical pain or overcoming bad habits. Learning steadfastness will also take us in unexpected directions as challenges refine our obedience. Wasn't that Peter's experience? He went from experiencing a miracle performed by Christ through his hands and nets to one performed through his preaching. Every trial thereafter motivated him to trust more in God's power.

If the Lord had spoken from the sky in those early days and told me to pastor a church, I would have screamed and run away. If I had tried to pastor a church out of sheer willpower, I would have collapsed and then screamed and run away. Instead, he encouraged me to do one thing—lead a Bible study—out of a sincere desire to follow him and with enough knowledge of the Bible to be useful. Breaking the bonds of my soul to old values and dreams was spaced out to encourage rather than discourage me. Through it all, a profound change was happening in who I was.

No, that's wrong; let me try that again. It didn't feel like I was changing. After that initial act of self-control, I felt like I was discovering who I really was. That's what learning steadfastness feels like when it's a product of grace, virtue, knowledge, and self-control. Try to push yourself into "the Christian life" outside of that progression, and it feels like you are trying to be someone else. Follow Jesus as Peter learned to follow him, and you discover what it truly means to be you.

The place of steadfastness in Peter's Principles (looking back to previous steps)

As with self-control, most Christians see steadfastness as sheer willpower, attempting to impress God, others, or ourselves. We think that way because we have not been trained in Peter's Principles, the dynamics of effective discipleship. Trying to jump from faith directly to steadfastness does not work well. Even if we modify an outward behavior, our inner desires and understanding remain untouched, and we are guaranteed frustration. We would be stapling fruit onto the vine. The fruit would be for show and would quickly wither. The truth is that our character cannot transform by simply willing ourselves to obey God's law.[8] Christians think this is what they are supposed to do because they haven't been instructed in the process that makes genuine obedience possible.

Peter tells us the process that works, the one Jesus used with him. Faith in Christ's saving grace is the prerequisite. God uses it to reconcile us to himself and give us a spiritually reborn heart confident in his perfect love, enjoying his presence, and anticipating a magnificent inheritance. Saving faith rests in the unchangeable love of God that is not threatened by our sins and failures. We do not change to impress God because we no longer need to impress God. Christ's character is credited to us 100%, and it doesn't get any better than that.

We seek personal character change when we see in Christ what we were made for and reach out to claim that which, by grace, already belongs to us. Then, when the passion for becoming what we are called to be is oriented to biblical truth, we attempt a concrete experience of self-control that does something we've never done before just because Jesus asks us to. Such an act of self-control is true obedience flowing out of saving faith, through our emotions (aspiration for virtue) and intellect (knowledge), to new behavior (self-control). Only then—when the change is something we genuinely want—are we ready to endure challenges that bake that new obedience into an increasingly Christ-like character.

No step can be skipped. Could a new character be formed apart from God's abundant grace? Could it exist without motivation? Could it be created without understanding? Will our character change if all we do is talk and never take the first step of obedience? The plain truth is that steadfast character change is impossible without every cylinder of Peter's Principles firing in concert. But when they do, progress in

---

[8] Romans 7:21-23.

character development is guaranteed, and we become more of the person God had in mind when he made us.

The place of steadfastness in Peter's Principles (looking forward to later steps)

Steadfastness is smack in the middle of Peter's seven steps, capping the first four necessary to cultivate a Christ-like character. Virtue, knowledge, self-control, and steadfastness provide the raw material for humility, gentleness, courage, contentment, honesty, and patience—all of Christ's inner qualities.

The three steps that follow switch gears to apply what we've learned. They describe the application of character in relationships. That is not obvious in the English word "godliness," and I will address that in the next chapter. The point is that after steadfastness, Peter's steps move from building a character engine to using that engine to create love.

The order of qualities in Peter's list implies that Christ-like love differs from the love we naturally experience. Our desires and convenience define the love that comes naturally. Who we love and what it means to love them is whatever we want it to mean. And we stop loving them whenever we don't feel like loving them anymore. Christ-like love is different because it honors God's design for relationships instead of our imagined convenience. Honoring God's design is a matter of character. That's why Peter does not speak of cultivating love until he first addresses character formation. Loving like Jesus requires the ability to adapt our character to honor God's design. We learn Christ-like love by applying the character of Christ to our relationships.

The relationship between character and love is no surprise to those familiar with the Old Testament. The Hebrew term that comes closest to the idea of God's love is *hesed*. It means faithfulness to our commitments and is based on God's character. It is God's character to keep his promise when he gives it. *Hesed* is typically translated as steadfast love. It is a commitment to faithfully live by the obligations our Creator designed for each relationship. This kind of love does not follow untethered feelings. Instead, it is a commitment to cultivate feelings appropriate to the relationship. Therefore, if our love is to become like Christ's, we must first learn the basic skills to develop steadfastness.

These two larger subdivisions of Peter's qualities—character and love—parallel the two aspects of God's nature that we were made to manifest. God is light.[9] He is righteous, just, holy, and everything good. This describes the redeemed *character* of his children. God is also love.[10] He is compassionate, merciful, fair, kind, and full of goodwill. This describes the redeemed *relationships* of God's children.

Peter shows that discipleship involves learning the ways of both light and love. Moreover, he shows how they are related to each other. Cultivating a character of light is necessary to develop relationships of love. We cannot become like Jesus any other way. This, too, is a critical insight into discipleship.

Steadfastness in the pursuit of Christ's mission

Christ's mission was not something he pursued in his spare time. His steadfast commitment was forged by everything that human sin, Satan's attack, and God's wrath would throw at him.[11] Bringing the kingdom of God into our fallen world was more than a full-time job for Jesus. It was who he was.

When we begin our journey of faith, we have little spiritual passion, knowledge, or self-control. Building God's kingdom seems separate and distinct from the rest of our lives. That's because it is; most of our lives are still shaped by our chaotic and sinful lifestyle before faith. The Cultural Mandate and the Great Commission seem like exotic projects to pursue in our free time.

But as we add to our faith in God's grace, we begin to discover in ourselves the people Jesus has called to life. Piece by piece and through many obstacles, steadfast changes repair

---

[9] 1 John 1:5-7.

[10] 1 John 4:15-16.

[11] Hebrews 5:7-8.

bits of our lifestyle to God's original design. As steadfast obedience expands into more areas, the Cultural Mandate and the Great Commission are no longer extras to pursue at our leisure. They become who we are. We bring the kingdom of God with us everywhere we go. It has become our mission, too.

§

Steadfastness connects character with relationships. When our awareness of grace, desire for virtue, and knowledge of God's will are all present, simple willpower can obey God through a new form of self-control. But character qualities like patience, honesty, loyalty, gentleness, kindness, and all the rest cannot develop as long as the focus remains on ourselves. They become real within relationships as we repeatedly exercise self-control through challenges and obstacles to craft love.

Peter next outlines how Christ-like love unfolds through three critical relationships.

Discussion Questions for Chapter 9

1. Share about something you have managed to learn (or are learning) even though it is challenging.
2. How is the biblical idea of steadfastness more than passive?
3. Describe how steadfastness is pictured by smelting and purifying ore.
   a) Which challenges in life can be used to develop steadfastness?
   b) Discuss the comment, "It is truly a shame when pain is wasted."
   c) Has Peter given any fresh insights into how we should encourage ourselves and others through trials?
4. How does steadfastness turn the mission to build God's kingdom from a project into our identity?

Chapter 10: Godliness

> For this very reason, make every effort to supplement your faith with virtue, and virtue with knowledge, and knowledge with self-control, and self-control with steadfastness, **and steadfastness with godliness**, and godliness with brotherly affection, and brotherly affection with love. (2 Peter 1:5-7)

Jesus' northern retreat with his disciples extended just into Gentile territory. It was one of the most important few weeks in Peter's life. That was when he became the first to confess that Jesus was the promised Christ. It was also when he saw divinity in Jesus.

Six days after Peter's confession, "Jesus took with him Peter and James, and John, his brother, and led them up a high mountain by themselves."[1] Jesus sometimes singled out these three disciples for special time with him. James would be the first to die for his witness to Christ. John would become the longest-living Apostle and receive Jesus' final revelation. And Peter … well, Peter was Peter, the "rock." The reason for his nickname became apparent during this trip.

On the mountain, Peter experienced what is called a theophany when God manifested his presence in creation. God exists everywhere but has chosen to display his presence locally on special occasions. Theophanies occurred on Mount

---

[1] Matthew 17:1.

Sinai with Moses and later with Elijah.[2] Moses was linked to the establishment of God's covenant, which was fulfilled in Jesus, and Elijah to announcing the fulfillment of God's covenant, as represented by John the Baptist.[3] Moses and Elijah each saw an overwhelming display of light from which God spoke to them. Now, Peter witnessed a theophany and understood the other figures present as Moses and Elijah.

This theophany was gloriously different, however. It wasn't that Moses, Elijah, Jesus, and his disciples experienced a theophany of God. Jesus *was* the theophany that the others experienced. Jesus was transformed into a manifestation of divinity. At the same time, the voice of God declared, "This is my beloved Son, with whom I am well pleased; listen to him."[4] Concepts like Trinity and incarnation were yet to be crisply defined, but Peter saw these truths before they were captured in words. He remembered every detail of that day for the rest of his life.[5]

It must have been difficult to obey Jesus' command to tell no one about what had happened. That frustration came to a head when they returned to Capernaum. Jews paid a yearly tax to support the Temple. It was collected by the money changers at the Temple when people visited during high feasts, but some collected it locally during the month leading up to a feast (in this case, Passover). The head of a household was responsible for the tax, and since Jesus lived in Peter's house, they approached Peter and asked if Jesus would pay it. The reason they asked was that Rabbis were exempt. Was Jesus claiming to be a Rabbi and therefore exempt? Peter had to say that Jesus did pay because religious leaders did not recognize him as a genuine Rabbi.

Given what Peter had recently seen, I put myself in Peter's shoes and imagine this felt humiliating. He was not at liberty to explain that Jesus was divine! Christ's relationship with

---

[2] Exodus 33:18-23; 1 Kings 19:9-18.
[3] Matthew 17:9-13.
[4] Matthew 17:5.
[5] 2 Peter 1:16-18.

God was unique, like that of a Son to a Father. And these bureaucrats expected him to pay tax for a Temple that already belonged to him!

What happened next must have become one of Peter's sweetest memories of Jesus. His Master had overheard the conversation and knew how ready to burst Peter must have felt, unable to tell these guys who his Master truly was. So before Peter could say anything, Jesus took the initiative ....

> And when [Peter] came into the house, Jesus spoke to him first, saying, "What do you think, Simon? From whom do kings of the earth take toll or tax? From their sons or from others?" And when he said, "From others," Jesus said to him, "Then the sons are free." (Matthew 17:25-26)

Jesus reassured Peter that he was indeed exempt from the tax, not because he was a Rabbi, but because he was the Son of God Peter confessed him to be. Then Jesus did something completely unnecessary. There is no reason to think they could not afford the two-drachma or half-shekel per person tax. But Jesus created a private joke just for frustrated Peter.

> However, not to give offense to them, go to the sea and cast a hook and take the first fish that comes up, and when you open its mouth you will find a shekel. Take that and give it to them for me and for yourself. (Matthew 17:27)

Jesus put Peter back on his boat for another miracle catch. Imagine how Peter felt as he quietly paid the tax with that particular shekel; the frustration of forced silence turned into the pride of a shared secret!

I wonder if it was then, or later, that Peter realized the significance of Jesus providing money to cover his tax, too. Jesus was saying that, as his disciple, Peter was also exempt. Why? Not because Peter was a Rabbi but because Jesus made him one of God's sons. "The sons are free." After the resurrection and the clarity of the Holy Spirit's arrival, Peter realized that although God loves only one *begotten* Son, he loves many *adopted* children. Jesus creates for us the same relationship with God the Father that he has.

The transfiguration and touching gesture with the fish together demonstrated divine holiness and compassion. As Isaiah had said,

> For thus says the One who is high and lifted up, who inhabits eternity, whose name is Holy: "I dwell in the high and holy place, and also with him who is of a contrite and lowly spirit, to revive the spirit of the lowly, and to revive the heart of the contrite." (Isaiah 57:15)

Before Jesus, Peter had a relationship with God that was only religious. Religion is a good teacher. However, the Lord wants more than formal religion, and so do we. In Jesus' character and love, Peter came to know God as a person. He is holy, wise, and utterly transcendent. But he also cares about hurtful conversations and crushed spirits. Christ ministered to Peter in a personalized and intimate way, not because it was necessary to accomplish his mission but because Jesus faithfully loved him. Although, come to think of it, I suppose faithful love was Jesus' mission.

Peter would eventually offer lifelong obedience to the Living God who, through Jesus, filled Peter's soul with transcendent purpose and deeply personal devotion—in Peter's words, "joy inexpressible and full of glory."[6]

§

Discipleship enables us to discover our true identity in Christ's character and love. At this point, Peter has already described four steps involved in expanding God's kingdom within our inner character. Now he applies that character to manifest the kingdom of God in our relationships. It may not be evident that Peter has turned such a corner because of a translation challenge involving *godliness*. We usually think of

---

[6] 1 Peter 1:8.

the word godliness as describing character. It does, but we miss the point if we do not see its connection with a relationship. So I will first examine what godliness is meant to convey and then return to this significant transition in Peter's Principles.

Godliness

The English word godliness translates the Greek word *eusebian*. For a Greek or Roman, this word described a nominally religious person who participated in the temple rites of one or more gods as a matter of good citizenship.

The Bible also describes a relationship with God modeled by religion but both more transcendent and imminent because it is based on personal loyalty to mutual promises. Relationships based on promises are called covenants. They cover everything from business contracts to marriage vows. The original covenant with Adam offered God's promise of eternal life in exchange for Adam's promise of trust and obedience. Adam rejected this covenant, resulting in death for him and all mankind.

The Old Testament then records a series of historical covenants God made with patriarchs like Abraham and eventually with the nation of Israel. These covenants reflected the same beneficial obligations as the first: God promised to provide a life of abundant blessing in exchange for the reasonable promise of trust and obedience. But they also included a new element: the offer of forgiveness for our failures to trust and obey. In other words, God offered eternal life to those who promised to trust and obey him while at the same time promising to forgive our failures. Both promises define this relationship. This covenant was made a reality when Jesus died in place of sinners, enabling God to forgive our sins. Since then, God has generously promised eternal life to anyone who promises to trust and obey his Son— understanding that all our failures to trust and obey have already been forgiven.

Surely this is the best deal ever, but only if it is understood. Some may ask God for salvation when they have no intention of trusting or obeying, assuming their sins will be forgiven. But it doesn't work that way. A saving relationship with God requires an honest promise to trust and obey Christ. God has no interest in saving people who have no desire to live where he is King. Our Creator wants heartfelt friendship and loyalty with people created to be in his image. Our promise must come from a heart brought to life by the Holy Spirit. God will forgive any number of failures if the intention to trust and obey is genuine.

This heartfelt commitment to trust, obey, honor, exalt, and please God is what the Old Testament understood as fearing and loving God:

> And now, Israel, what does the LORD your God require of you, but to fear the LORD your God, to walk in all his ways, to love him, to serve the LORD your God with all your heart and with all your soul. (Deuteronomy 10:12)

The Old Testament *fear God* is translated in Peter's text as *godliness*. Godliness refers to loving God with all our heart and soul by genuinely wanting to walk in his ways. It is the character trait of steadfast obedience applied to our relationship with God.

Note the difference between this step and the four others before it. Up to now, character development has involved working with the Holy Spirit on issues primarily within myself. Godliness, however, moves in a new direction. Godliness is the first example of character development initiated for a specific relationship. It uses the character skills I've developed thus far to intentionally develop faithful love for God. Later steps in Peter's Principles expand this to love for fellow Christians (brotherly affection) and then love for everyone.

Before he met Christ, Peter would have understood the idea of godliness as a religious reverence and obedience. But on the mountain and later with the tax collectors, godliness became personal because God became personal. Peter began to sense what Abraham and Moses must have felt when

Almighty God called them his friends.[7] The obedience God required of those two was striking, but their friendship with God was beyond price. In fact, friends are precisely what Jesus called his disciples when they gathered for their last meal together:

> This is my commandment, that you love one another as I have loved you. Greater love has no one than this, that someone lay down his life for his friends. You are my friends if you do what I command you. No longer do I call you servants, for the servant does not know what his master is doing; but I have called you friends, for all that I have heard from my Father I have made known to you. (John 15:12-15)

Love for God is friendship with God. But God's friendship is unlike any other, for he is God; we are not. That is why Jesus linked his friendship with obedience. Required obedience in one direction would usually be strange between two human friends, but it is necessary between God and those created to reflect his image and likeness. Jesus explicitly tied intimacy with him and his Heavenly Father with our obedience:

> If anyone loves me, he will keep my word, and my Father will love him, and we will come to him and make our home with him. Whoever does not love me does not keep my words. And the word that you hear is not mine but the Father's who sent me. (John 14:23-24)

Godliness begins a new segment within Peter's sequence. It's still about character, but now the focus is on adapting our character to love as Christ loves. And the first one we must learn to love is God. It may not be evident that we must *learn* to love God because we spontaneously feel positive emotions toward him in worship. However, those feelings are only as meaningful as our loyalty and obedience.

---

[7] 2 Chronicles 20:7; Isaiah 41:8; James 2:23.

My story

I began to love God the way most do, through the religion he gave us. Most religions are man-made idolatry.[8] But the Lord gave us details of a religion that represents him well, detailed to Israel in the Old Testament with principles applied to believers from every race in the New Testament. The Church's liturgy taught me the language of divine friendship: reverence, praise, humility, gratitude, peace, and joy.

God saw love in my obedience to submit to the religion he gave us. My first official act of obedience was my baptism. Then I learned to dedicate to God one day in seven and gather with others to celebrate the great themes of redemption. Obeying the Lord's will to participate in those things was the beginning of my love for him.

In worship, the Church keeps it simple and basic, almost always addressing God as Father or Lord. Those two roles are rich with mutual promises that define friendship with God. Besides giving me life, my Heavenly Father loves me by faithfully caring for me, providing for me, and adopting me into his family. I love him by living in a manner worthy of his name, using his provision well, and rejoicing in his affection. I understood something about this relationship because I had a human father and only needed to adjust my notion of fatherhood around the character of God revealed in his Word.

However, relating to God as Lord was more difficult. I didn't have experience dealing with a King since I don't live under a monarchy. I call God my King and Christ my Lord, but what does that mean? How should it feel? What mutual commitments are implied by such a relationship? The closest non-father authority role I could relate to was Supervisor or Boss. I remembered what it felt like to enter my first supervisor's office, so in prayer one morning, I imagined walking into God's office with a list of things I wanted to discuss with him.

---

[8] Romans 1:18-25.

That is when I first saw God's wisdom in likening himself to human roles that we understand. As I thought of God using the role of Boss, I began to relate to him in new ways. First, the size of his desk reminded me that the scope of his concerns is much larger than mine. His authority not only covers what I bring to him but also extends far beyond that to cover many other people and projects. Then I realized he also had a list of things in his hand that he wanted to discuss with me! That made me realize how flippantly I sometimes used "Lord" in my prayers. Why would I think I would monopolize a conversation with my Boss (let alone Lord or King), and the only things we would discuss were what I wanted to talk about? With my Heavenly Dad, I could bring up anything, anytime. But with my Boss? No, I realized that we would first discuss the items on his mind: his vision for the business, my job description, how my training and projects were going, how I was doing, and how he could help me thrive in my work. Since my recent reading of Scripture had highlighted some things on his mind, that's where we started.

By then, some of the items on my list had already been dealt with, others did not need to be raised, and he was very interested in listening to my ideas as I brought up what was left. Faithfully working for God as a wonderful Boss/Lord enhances my appreciation of both his transcendence over me and intimacy with me. I'm learning to live with the Friend who is not my equal but my Lord.

Scriptural Roles of God

I learn to obey God intelligently through his commandments and biblical narratives. But over time and the study of Scripture, I began to see that God also explained his desired relationship with us through a number of familiar roles and metaphors. Whenever I trust God to be like one of these roles and choose to live assuming that is true, I add depth and sincerity to my obedience.

God's roles help us relate to God. We cannot see God directly. We can only see God through his creation and the history of redemption, which culminated in Jesus Christ.[9] To help us relate to him, God has likened himself to many people and things we have experienced. God is light. God is a rock. God is a fortress. God is a mighty warrior. God is a king. God is a father. Add together God's many compound names and likenesses to familiar social characters like doctors and lawyers, along with a host of metaphors, and believers can apply abundant life experience to know God better.

God's roles tell us how to trust and obey God. The more we know who God is, the better we can obey him. Every way God uses to describe himself implies a promise. For example, since the Bible describes God as a Shepherd, we may assume that he promises to shepherd us. Since God is light, he promises to illuminate us. The fact that God consistently acts in accordance with who he is makes every biblical description of God a promise. I need only take care to understand each role as the Bible applies it.

God's promises fill out his side of the loving relationship he desires to share with us. We learn to love God by trusting that God is who he says he is and living responsively (in obedience). Since the Lord is my Shepherd, I obey by following him in paths of righteousness and trusting him to search for me when I don't follow well. Since God is my Light, I trust him to reveal the nature of reality, and I obey by living accordingly to what he reveals.

God's roles reveal my intended identity. The better I trust and obey God in his many roles, the better I understand who he designed me to be in the world he made. Is God a king? I am his royal child. Is God living water? I drink deeply of his grace and pass it along to other thirsty souls.

As I have contemplated God's many roles, I am struck by how they instruct my emotions every bit as much as my intellectual understanding. God is inherently holy, separate, and unknowable in any direct sense. Yet, by giving us a host of similarities that I am familiar with, God teaches me how he feels about me and how I should feel about him. When I trust

---

[9] Psalm 19; John 1:18.

in God's roles, part of obedience is to rest in God's emotions toward me and reflect them back appropriately and enthusiastically.

Therefore, it isn't necessary for me to *only* speak to God as my Heavenly Father. That will probably always be my favorite "go-to" role, but God has described himself in many other ways, some related to the Godhead as a whole and some specific to the Father, Son, or Holy Spirit. Here is a small handful of examples:

- Bridegroom - Hosea 2:19-20; John 3:28-29
- Painter, sculptor, and gardener of the Earth
  - Psalm 104; Isaiah 64:8
- Redeemer, purchasing my freedom - Galatians 3:13; 1 Corinthians 7:21-23
- Military General - Joshua 5:15-15
- Teacher - Matthew 23:8-10
- Judge - Acts 17:30-31; 1 Peter 2:21-25
- Mighty one, valiant hero - Isaiah 9:6
- Shepherd - Psalm 23; John 10:1-18
- Brother - Romans 8:29; Hebrews 2:14-18
- Gardener - John 15:1-8; Isaiah 5:1-7
- Architect and builder of the church - Matthew 16:18; Ephesians 2:17-22
- Helper - Psalm 54:4; John 14:16,26
- Coach - Hebrews 12:1-2

Add to these a ton of divine names and metaphors. We can use each biblical role to expand our repertoire of worship, prayer, and the slices of life we experience with him. To see what I mean, try confessing the same sin to God five times, approaching him sequentially in his roles of Father, King, Judge, Teacher, and Coach.

Because God's roles train my obedience, they enhance the transcendent side of our relationship. Because they model my identity, they enhance the immanent side. When I integrate these roles into worship, my relationship with God deepens. Sin, grace, commitment, loyalty, love, and mission take on weight and become more three-dimensional. I'll never forget the first time I prayed to God as the King of Glory, mighty in battle.[10] I stood at attention, repeating his commandments to confirm my understanding, and ended with, "Yes, Sir!" Try it, and say it out loud like you mean it!

As we explore God's many biblical roles, obedience feels less like following rules and more like discovering ourselves in service to an ever-more-glorious Friend.

The place of loving God in Peter's Principles

Understanding godliness in terms of loving God reveals a profound pattern in Peter's Principles. The first four steps build character, and the last three steps build relationships. Since he intentionally places the steps in order, Peter tells us that *learning to love depends on character development*. It is good to praise God spontaneously, but Christ-like love for God is steadfast, faithful, and shaped by God's revealed will. This kind of love does not just happen. Love for God must be learned by adjusting my thoughts, feelings, and behavior according to God's design for our relationship.

That requires strength of character, and Peter tells me how to develop it. I start with saving faith, then let God's grace overflow in aspiration to share his goodness, then gain Bible knowledge to know what that involves, then do something I've never done before just because Jesus wants me to do it, and then develop endurance by maintaining that obedience through trials and challenges. Each cycle through Peter's Principles increases the range of my obedience and my delight in God's friendship. I can do this over and over throughout the rest of my life.

God's love for me is assured because his faithfulness is perfect, Christ's redemption is accomplished, and his affections are forever settled. But my love for God can be perfected to become more and more worthy of what he

---

[10] Psalm 24:7-8.

deserves. Receiving God's love for me requires only a passive trust in Christ. To love God, however, requires that I make every effort to add to my faith—a labor of love stretching from what I feel to what I understand to what I do.

Of course, we cannot love God perfectly in this life. This would be a problem if his love depended on ours or if seeking to love him were a chore or burden. But neither is true. God's redemptive love in Christ is unconditional, and our yearning to love him better is a hunger and thirst that God loves to satisfy.[11] He delights in our efforts to grow in steadfast love for him because they demonstrate the impact of his Son's work for us and his Spirit's work in us, which makes him very happy indeed.

Love for God in the pursuit of Christ's mission

Our relationship with God is at the beginning of learning how to love. Peter goes on to talk about love for our spiritual family (Christ's Church) and love for everyone (all our neighbors), but love for God must come first. Over the years, I have been struck by how easy it is to forget that. As a pastor, my ministry most naturally springs from a love for God's people, the brotherly affection Peter mentions next. I know gifted evangelists whose ministry most naturally springs from a love for those who do not yet know Christ. But neither of those loves provides an adequate foundation for ministry because just as there is a natural flow to building character, there is also a natural flow to cultivating love. Love for people, whether Christian or non-Christian, must be an overflow of our love for God, or it will become imbalanced, warped, unhealthy—an idol. The healthiest, strongest, and purist love for people is a consequence of loving God with all our heart, mind, soul, and strength.

Let me illustrate this from Christ's life. At the beginning of his ministry, immediately after his Father's voice from heaven declared pleasure in Jesus at his baptism, Satan tempted Christ

---

[11] Matthew 5:6.

to take a shortcut to his own glory by worshiping him.[12] Christ would have none of it. The God-Man knew who he was and knew that he had come with the single overarching purpose to glorify his Father by accomplishing his will. That is God's overarching purpose for every human being.

Jesus revisited the same issue as he finally approached the cross:

> And they went to a place called Gethsemane. And he said to his disciples, "Sit here while I pray." And he took with him Peter and James and John, and began to be greatly distressed and troubled. And he said to them, "My soul is very sorrowful, even to death. Remain here and watch." And going a little farther, he fell on the ground and prayed that, if it were possible, the hour might pass from him. And he said, "Abba, Father, all things are possible for you. Remove this cup from me. Yet not what I will, but what you will." (Mark 14:32-36)

We are meant to see here something we may not be comfortable seeing. In the end, Jesus did not go to the cross to save the world or even to save those who believed in him. Jesus indeed loves us and died on our behalf, but in the end, he did not decide to go to the cross because he loved us. He went to the cross because he loved his Father. If there had been any other way to please and glorify his Father, he would have taken it. There wasn't. So for his Father's sake, Jesus wrapped himself around his Father's love for us and went to the cross. That is what loving God means; it shows that love for people flows from an overflowing love for God.

Basing kingdom ministry on love for the Church will ultimately miss the mark. It is only a matter of time before we confuse making disciples of Christ with something else, such as excitement, numbers, money, or prestige. Basing kingdom ministry on love for those still lost will ultimately miss the mark. Again, it is only a matter of time before we confuse making disciples of Christ with something else, such as

---

[12] Luke 4:1-13.

making a name for ourselves or compromising the message for the sake of results.

A healthy love for the Church and our neighbors is the overflow of love for God. Look at how Peter understands both the significance of the Church and the nature of evangelism in terms of God's glory:

> But you are a chosen race, a royal priesthood, a holy nation, a people for his own possession, that you may proclaim the excellencies of him who called you out of darkness into his marvelous light. (1 Peter 2:9)

The Church is a people for God's own possession. Evangelism proclaims the excellencies of him who called us into his light. If we are to pursue Christ's mission, we will indeed need to love the Church and love our neighbors. But such love will only be sustained, guided, empowered, and safe when—like Jesus in his humanity—our love begins with God.

§

As our love for God grows, we will develop the hunger and capacity to apply our growing Christ-likeness to the next fundamental relationship of the Christian's life, the Church.

Discussion Questions for Chapter 10

1. Read Isaiah 57:15 (quoted in the chapter). Where do you find it harder to relate to God: in the high and holy place or as one lowly of spirit?
2. How do you feel about the idea that love for God is expressed by obeying him?
3. The Bible says that God has many roles in our lives.
   a) Share one that is particularly meaningful to you.
   b) Is there a role of God that you would like to explore?
4. Peter says that love for the Church and for our neighbors grow out of our love for God. Why is love for God foundational?

Chapter 11: Brotherly Affection

> For this very reason, make every effort to supplement your faith with virtue, and virtue with knowledge, and knowledge with self-control, and self-control with steadfastness, and steadfastness with godliness, **and godliness with brotherly affection**, and brotherly affection with love. (2 Peter 1:5-7)

At Pentecost, three thousand people declared their faith in Jesus. They were baptized and became Christians before anyone had invented the word. Instantly, everything changed. Until then, "the disciples" had been a definite and contained group. Peter knew each of the 120 people who had gathered that morning to pray. By the end of the day, however, the church had multiplied 25 times! Never again would Peter personally know every follower of Jesus.

Even so, it was imperative that they develop a relationship with each other. During his last supper with his disciples, Jesus said that mutual love would be the distinguishing characteristic of his followers.[1] More than that, their mutual love was essential for kingdom growth.

> I do not ask for these only, but also for those who will believe in me through their word, that they may all be one, just as you, Father, are in me, and I in you, that they also

---

[1] John 13:34-35.

may be in us, so that the world may believe that you have sent me ...

I in them and you in me, that they may become perfectly one, so that the world may know that you sent me and loved them even as you loved me. (John 17:20-21,23)

If kingdom expansion depended on mutual love between Christians, how would this love develop among the growing thousands? When considering this, Peter must have remembered how Jesus dealt with large crowds by dividing them into manageable groups.[2] Peter's straightforward application of that technique changed the world.

And they devoted themselves to the apostles' teaching and the fellowship, to the breaking of bread and the prayers. And awe came upon every soul, and many wonders and signs were being done through the apostles. And all who believed were together and had all things in common. And they were selling their possessions and belongings and distributing the proceeds to all, as any had need. And day by day, attending the temple together and breaking bread in their homes, they received their food with glad and generous hearts, praising God and having favor with all the people. And the Lord added to their number day by day those who were being saved. (Acts 2:42-47)

Almost overnight, dozens of homes were recruited. I assume Peter was critical in this process because he had personal experience using his home to host Jesus and his followers. Now, dozens of homes hosted Jesus (through the Holy Spirit) and his followers. History calls them house churches, and it was how Christians met for two and a half centuries.

In those house churches, the apostles taught what Jesus had taught them. They prayed together and sought God's presence and power together. They were used to meeting for worship in the Temple, so they knew that those who worshiped the Lord were members of his kingdom. But now,

---

[2] Luke 9:10-17.

they worshiped in homes and began to experience life as God's family.[3] Rich and poor met together. Slaves and free citizens met together. Men and women met together. Their common faith and home-based experience made their relationship that of brothers.[4]

To the outside observer, the most remarkable evidence of this brotherhood was how Christians shared their material resources. People did not typically offer financial aid to others, but sharing resources with Christians in need became a defining characteristic of knowing Jesus.[5] In the larger culture, sharing resources was not uncommon among families, of course. But these Christians had been strangers before their faith. Faith in Jesus had made them a real family.

Then just as Peter was getting used to helping Jewish strangers become brothers in Christ (the entire church was still Jewish at this time), there arose the new challenge of ethnic diversity:

> Now in these days when the disciples were increasing in number, a complaint by the Hellenists arose against the Hebrews because their widows were being neglected in the daily distribution. (Acts 6:1)

The early church pooled resources to help Christian widows because that's what a family does. But there were two kinds of Jews and two kinds of widows. The "Hebrews" had been raised locally and held to the old Jewish ways. The "Hellenists" were also Jews but had adopted Greek practices (Greek was the universal Mediterranean culture). They shared the same race and religious heritage but represented different ethnicities. The complaint was that the Hebraic widows got preferential treatment.

This first internal challenge to the new Christian Church was about diversity and whether one ethnic group would be

---

[3] Galatians 6:10; Ephesians 2:19; 1 Timothy 3:15.

[4] From the beginning, the term "brothers" or "brethren" in this context applied to both men and women.

[5] 1 John 3:14-18.

favored over another. How could Christ's command to "love one another" be a unique witness if Christians loved each other pretty much the same way other people loved each other, in other words, by only loving people like them?

Peter's solution was revolutionary. He organized the selection of six men of good spiritual reputations who were entrusted with the task of distributing aid.[6] They were the Church's first official "servants." That role was eventually formalized using the Greek word for servant to create the office of Deacon. What was revolutionary was that the men chosen for the task all had *Greek* names. In other words, members from the minority group were entrusted with ensuring fairness. That decision and its outcome were so incredibly impressive to onlookers that many priests serving when Jesus was crucified became believers.[7] Sensitively and fairly resolving conflict, even across ethnic boundaries, became a mark of Christian love that convinced people that Jesus had founded the kingdom of God for all the world.[8]

Jesus had foreseen the new spiritual family Peter would guide. Once, an interested young man declined to follow Jesus because of his greater love for wealth and status. To his disciples afterward, Jesus made his famous comment about rich men, camels, and the eyes of needles. Peter responded by immediately pointing out how he and the others had left everything to follow the Master.

> Jesus said, "Truly, I say to you, there is no one who has left house or brothers or sisters or mother or father or children or lands, for my sake and for the gospel, who will not receive *a hundredfold now in this time, houses and brothers and sisters and mothers and children and lands*, with persecutions, and in the age to come eternal life." (Mark 10:29-30, *emphasis added*)

---

[6] Acts 6:1-6.

[7] Acts 6:7.

[8] For another example, see Acts 4:32-33.

Perhaps on that day, Peter expected his wife to bear many children, and they would enjoy the wealth of many properties. But that's not the way it turned out. Peter's calling to put Christ first cost him everything, including the prosperity he once sought in his fishing business.

But a strange thing happened as he reconfigured his life around Jesus, and his love for God grew. Wherever Peter went preaching Christ, he found strangers who loved Jesus as he did, and they would share with him their homes, their food, and all they had. They gave him love generally reserved for extended family. That was because, in Christ, they *were* an extended spiritual family. Instead of knowing the comfort of only one home, Peter gained hundreds. Instead of one set of parents and children, he gained more than he could count. Jesus' promise to Peter was fulfilled in the Church.

§

Discipleship equips me to find my identity in the character and love of Christ. The first kind of love we build with Christ-like character is for God, shaping our lives around who he is. The second kind of love is with other believers, shaping our lives around who they are in Christ.

We know that there are other Christians in the world, and we are probably part of a church with a number of them. But often, except for our personal friends, the other worshippers are like strangers who share the same elevator. Nice people, no doubt, who look very much like us and share the same destination. Still, they are strangers, so we stare straight ahead, interacting only to be polite. And if people who look or sound different from us enter our elevator car, there is an uncomfortable silence even though they are going to the same floor. Perhaps they should take another elevator.

Things begin to change, however, when I use my developing character skills to reshape my relationship with God according to who he is. My experience of his Fatherhood expands as he helps me make choices that make him proud.

His Kingly power calms my anxiety and appoints ways to build his kingdom that give me purpose. As my Shepherd, he rescues me from bad choices and carries me back home, turning old scars into souvenirs of his intervention. The more I reshape my life around the roles God used to describe our relationship, the more my love for him grows.

As my friendship with God develops, I realize I am not the only one he loves. Other Christians, including many I don't know, are experiencing the same God I experience. The more of my life I share with God, the more I have in common with them. The Apostle John described what is happening:

Everyone who believes that Jesus is the Christ has been born of God, and everyone who loves the Father loves whoever has been born of him. (1 John 5:1)

If God is *my* Heavenly Father and *your* Heavenly Father, then we must be spiritual siblings. As I grow in my identity as God's child, I cannot help but become more and more aware that I am your brother in Christ and that you are my brother or sister. That awareness begins as a theological fact, but the more I experience love for God, the more my connection to fellow Christians becomes real. Our family ties are reinforced as I learn to love God through his many roles. We not only share the same Father but the same Shepherd, the same King, the same Teacher, the same Healer, and on and on. As I spend time with God in all these different roles, I keep running into these same people!

Again, we see how Peter arranged his seven steps intentionally. An overflowing love for God naturally flows into love for other believers. Jesus said that we love God by obeying him joyfully and treating him as the God he truly is. As this love overflows, I treat other Christians as they truly are —my spiritual family, fellow citizens, sheep of the same flock, other stones in the Temple, teammates in sports, etc. Peter characterizes the love for fellow believers as *brotherly affection*.

The most enjoyable experience of brotherly affection has to be Christian friendship. Two people who are Christians can experience natural friendship the same way anyone experiences friendship, perhaps by sharing things like fishing or tennis. However, two Christians can also experience a spiritual dimension. A common devotion to Christ can create a Christian friendship that takes the relationship to another level.

Many Christian friendships develop through small groups or ministry programs. A shared experience with Jesus (our mutual friend) raises natural friendships into spiritual ones that include Christ. Spiritual friendships are extremely important for continued growth in Christ.

> Let us hold fast the confession of our hope without wavering, for he who promised is faithful. And let us consider how to stir up one another to love and good works, not neglecting to meet together, as is the habit of some, but encouraging one another, and all the more as you see the Day drawing near. (Hebrews 10:23-25)

We must understand, however, that brotherly affection is not limited to Christian friendship. We know this because brotherly affection highlights a different kind of relationship, that of family. People become *friends* because they like each other. They choose each other because of similar social demographics or mutual interests. When it comes to *family*, however, no such choice is possible. Family is about the common identity of people who share the same roots by genetics or adoption, the same home, name, and heritage. Family bonds are naturally powerful. I have a brother ten years older than I am. We live 1,000 miles apart and only communicate a few times each year. We are not friends in the sense of doing things we enjoy together. But if needed, we would be there for each other. Why? Because we are family.

As we reshape our lives around God, the bonds between Christians become more like family. A shared identity develops between people who do not choose each other but who participate in the same life in Christ. The more our love for God grows, the more we are conscious of our spiritual family ties. We share the same spiritual heritage; Abraham,

Moses, Esther, Daniel, Mary, and Peter are our common spiritual ancestors. We share the same name, "Christian." People who share all this may or may not spontaneously enjoy each other as friends, but they will grow to love each other as a spiritual family.

Christians needed a word to describe how their common faith in Christ connected them. In the Roman and Greek cultures, relationships usually paralleled recognized social ties like the natural family or the military. However, there was one other sort of bond. People in similar businesses or professions sometimes formed guilds and partnerships to pursue common business concerns. Unlike other social groups, these people were related by a common vocation. They were not in the same physical family. They did not live together and might not share the same social circles. They had not necessarily chosen each other as friends. Instead, they had a common commitment that linked them independently of the things that generally tie people together. Christians adopted their word for business partnerships to describe Christian relationships. *Koinonia* is usually translated in English as "fellowship." *Koinonia* expresses the bond between everyone who has faith in Jesus, a bond that creates a spiritual family regardless of social differences or personal friendship.

Christian fellowship is not natural

To appreciate what Christian fellowship is, it's helpful to understand what it is not.

Christian fellowship is not the relationship between Christian members of the same natural family. Often, members of the same household are Christians, and Christian fellowship is layered over their natural family connection. But the two layers are distinct. When Peter speaks of brotherly affection, he is not talking about natural ties with literal siblings. Such bonds are great, but they are not *koinonia*. I can have brotherly affection for someone in my birth family who is a Christian. But I can have the same brotherly affection for Christians outside my birth family. This is not natural.

Christian fellowship is not friendship. Friendships among Christians are sweet and necessary for spiritual growth. Apart from sharing a common faith, friends choose each other because they like each other. *Koinonia,* however, has to do with what binds us as believers, not what draws us to each other as friends. In time, sharing the same faith will often cause Christians to become friends, but *koinonia,* or fellowship, connects every Christian whether or not they are friends or happen to like each other. This is not natural.

Christian fellowship is unnatural because it has nothing to do with the social connections that typically bind us to others. Christians are in *koinonia* with each other because of a shared life in Christ—a common union with Jesus forged by a common gospel faith—guaranteeing the same eternal future. In some ways, we have more in common with Christian strangers, however socially distant from us, than with our closest friend or dearest relative who does not know Christ.

Sharing bonds with Christian strangers that are more profound than our bonds with non-Christian family and friends is not natural, but Jesus insisted that faith in him creates a deeper bond than we have with our physical family.[9] Any two people with a high commitment to Christ inevitably share a unique relationship. It's not like a birth family. It's not friendship. It's *koinonia.* Through the Book of Acts, *koinonia* has remarkably practical manifestations. People open their homes and use resources to care for people they genuinely love *only* because they both love Jesus.

When Christian faith is mustard seed size, we use familiar cultural affinities to explore fellowship—common interests or common seasons of life. The resulting friendships become valued treasures. But the more we find our true identity in Christ, the more we identify with others who know Jesus regardless of cultural similarities. For example, in the New Testament church, the enslaved and the free worshipped together. Paul reminded one Christian slave owner to treat his now-Christian runaway slave as a brother.

---

[9] Matthew 10:34-39; Luke 9:57-62.

> For this perhaps is why he was parted from you for a while, that you might have him back forever, no longer as a bondservant but more than a bondservant, as a beloved brother. (Philemon 1:15-16)

Paul did not have the authority to abolish the world's structures, but he taught that a family relationship should exist between people who both find their identity in Christ. That *koinonia* is more profound than the factors that socially divide us.

Brotherly affection goes even further. Not only does it love other Christians across social boundaries, but it also loves other Christians despite all manner of conflict. Christian brothers and sisters hurt each other. (That is another way the Church is like a natural family.) But while natural families are famous for wounds that never heal, Christ teaches us to behave differently in the household of God. Christian brothers are taught to forgive each other.

> Then Peter came up and said to him, "Lord, how often will my brother sin against me, and I forgive him? As many as seven times?" Jesus said to him, "I do not say to you seven times, but seventy-seven times." (Matthew 18:21-22)

A similar passage in Luke says the two can reconcile if the sinning brother repents.[10] The above passage in Matthew 18 does not mention repentance and restoration, but only forgiveness. Reconciliation is always the goal, but Christ teaches us to have a forgiving spirit regardless of whether the one who offends us has repented. Persistent goodwill and affection throughout conflict are not natural, but they exist wherever Christians have a love for God that is stronger than their conflict.

---

[10] Luke 17:3-4.

My story

I found Christ through a university Christian fellowship and a local church filled with people who were pretty much like me: middle-class, white, and suburban. Most of my time was spent with my college fellowship, so we were all about the same age and single. I made dear friends, some of whom I continue in fellowship with to this day. I knew that all kinds of other Christians existed worldwide, but I had no sense of a relationship with them.

That began to change when I participated in the 1970 InterVarsity missions conference in Urbana, Illinois. It turned out to be one of the high points of my life. What Urbana did was to open my mind and my heart to the breadth of Christ's people. Eleven thousand students came from all over the world. I had never been exposed to so many languages and cultures. Part of what made it easy was that we were all students and had much in common. We listened to the same messages and studied the same gospel. A Chinese student came to faith in my small group, and I saw Christ working in his life as he worked in mine. When we sang together, those eleven thousand voices welcomed me into a genuinely international fellowship. It forever changed my notion of the kingdom of God.

The next thing that opened my eyes to my spiritual family was experiencing different churches. I had a home evangelical church. I also spent a year and a half in a charismatic church in Boston that sponsored a house community where Christian students lived with an elder and wife as mentors and chaperones. Then I pursued my pastoral internship in a Baptist congregation. Finally, I was ordained in my Reformed and Presbyterian fellowship. While this was just a tiny taste of the larger Church, it helped me sense *koinonia* with people who love Jesus across different church backgrounds.

My next awakening to fellowship occurred when, at age 25, I became the Pastor of my first church. Those were the days when people expected home visits from the Pastor, and I was out visiting several nights a week, every week. This put me into contact with Christians who were the age of my parents and grandparents and also with children and infants. I spent several years ministering at three local nursing homes and had the opportunity to get to know Christians who were disabled. I found that Jesus can live in people of any age or state of health.

In my second church, where I served for almost 40 years, I had the privilege of helping two Korean-speaking congregations get their start in our facilities before securing a permanent meeting place. The simple experience of hearing sermons and prayers in a different language expanded my sense of God's family.

More recently, I've become aware that in many countries, Christians do not receive a fair share of aid sent during catastrophes, so I have targeted some of my giving to specifically aid my larger Christian family.[11] These people are not Indians or Sudanese who happen to be Christian. They are my Christian family who happen to live in India or Sudan.

Looking back, I wish I had been intentionally discipled to develop my experience of *koinonia* more fully. My capacity to love the brethren has been hindered by a lack of intentional exposure to broader Christianity and my failure to seek it out more. Even so, whenever I'm welcomed by anyone who loves Jesus, I sense that I'm home.

I have not survived fifty-three years as a Christian and forty-four in pastoral ministry without conflict. I particularly remember the attempt by a church leader to instigate a congregational rebellion against me, a lawsuit against the church stemming from charges of misconduct from a member of my pastoral staff, a suit for twenty million dollars brought directly against me from a man under church discipline, a threat to my life which called for armed protection, and an internet smear campaign designed to destroy my reputation. Such situations are not unique to the Church, of course. Christians deal with the same conflicts as non-Christians.

---

[11] One such ministry is www.barnabasaid.org/us/.

I've learned that when I willingly follow Jesus into the pain of his people, I discover my weaknesses in them—the same rationalizations, blindness to internal faults, and desperate attempts to "win" that only perpetuate loss for everyone. When I follow Jesus into pain, I rediscover how much I needed to be saved in the first place and how much Jesus patiently loves me.

I've learned that it's easy to take offense and look away from other Christians' pain unless I see these people as God's children and my brothers and sisters, fathers and mothers, sons and daughters. I've learned the value of involving experienced believers to help me in reconciliation. I've learned that my relational problems are not only the other person's fault. I've learned to listen when people throw their anguish in my direction and beware of my flaws as we clean up the mess. I've learned that even though I am a counselor, I need counsel, and even though I help others deal with all kinds of stress, I need help with my own.

Some of the hurts are still sore. But this is the household of God, and I am determined to see everyone who loves Jesus as my family because I know Jesus loves them as much as he loves me.

So what happened to fellowship?

Most religions require new believers to accept that religion's culture of origin. A unique strength of Christianity is that, since the culture that spawned it (Old Testament Judaism) is extinct, every culture receives Christ on equal terms, learning from the same Old and New Testaments and adapting their expression of faith to local culture. This makes Christianity genuinely multicultural.

On the other hand, once the Christian faith settles in a particular culture, local believers have difficulty separating their culture's flavor from the essence of faith. The result is that Christians divide fellowship along cultural and social lines. Such tribal identity is natural and adds variety and spice. The downside, however, is that *koinonia* gives ground in the Church to divisions of social standing, nationality, political affinity, and race.

This is certainly true within American Christianity. We select our churches to be with people with whom we are most comfortable. This is natural. Within our congregations, we are most committed to those who are personal friends or would likely be our friends if we had the opportunity. These are the people we generally care about, greet, pray for, and do things with. This is entirely natural.

The problem is that emphasizing so much that is natural leaves very little room for *koinonia*.

> For if you love those who love you, what reward do you have? Do not even the tax collectors do the same? And if you greet only your brothers, what more are you doing than others? Do not even the Gentiles do the same? You therefore must be perfect, as your heavenly Father is perfect. (Matthew 5:45-48)

The above quote from the Sermon on the Mount describes life in the kingdom of God. God's kingdom does not wipe out my natural affections or make them less precious. But in the kingdom of God, I'm called to cultivate a common identity with others who share the same blood (Christ's), the same spirit (the Holy one), the same mandate (the Cultural one), the same commission (a Great one), and the same future (an everlasting one). Other Christians may or may not become my friends, but they need to become something different and more profound than friends. They need to become *brethren*, my Christian brothers and sisters.

The word "fellowship" has come to mean socializing with Christians most like us. But true fellowship, or *koinonia*, cuts across social boundaries:

> ... in Christ Jesus you are all sons of God, through faith. For as many of you as were baptized into Christ have put on Christ. There is neither Jew nor Greek, there is neither slave nor free, there is no male and female, for you are all one in Christ Jesus. (Galatians 3:26-28)

Paul's reference to male and female reminds me to clarify that when I speak of relating to the diversity of my spiritual family, I am referring to differences that generally have nothing to do with our choice. Paul mentions race, slavery, and gender as examples. (Later in the book, I will address the contemporary notion of crafting our identity artificially.)

Relational conflicts are even more divisive. When a church experiences conflict, how many Christians become part of the problem, and how many become part of the solution? How many abandon the congregation without even trying to reconcile? Stirring up discord in God's family is Satan's lazy way of attacking us—we do all the work.

Beyond our local church, we seem eager to bury brotherly affection beneath cultural divisions that define us by dividing us. In today's toxic atmosphere, we see this most clearly in politics. The trend is to care more about those we are connected to politically than for our Christian family on the other side. Just think for a minute about trying to justify that to Jesus.

Dealing with conflict is a major theme of the Lord's Prayer and the Sermon on the Mount. Many of Jesus' applications in the Sermon on the Mount relate to forgiveness and reconciliation. Jesus' most famous teaching about prayer includes:

> and forgive us our debts, as we also have forgiven our debtors ...
>
> For if you forgive others their trespasses, your heavenly Father will also forgive you, but if you do not forgive others their trespasses, neither will your Father forgive your trespasses. (Matthew 6:12,14-15)

Jesus will not accept people as his disciples who consciously and persistently refuse to forgive and avoid reconciliation with other believers. This is echoed in the rest of the New Testament and is something we desperately need to realize.[12] Brotherly affection embraces a forgiving spirit and desire to be reconciled because it is built on Christians' shared experience of God's forgiveness.

In the American church, what happened to biblical *koinonia*? We care for Christians who look like us, talk like us, and share our opinions, but not so much for those who don't. We prefer to relate almost exclusively along national and racial borders. Even in the local church, we gravitate toward people of the same age, same interests, same life situations, and same social and political perspective—the rest we treat with benign indifference.

My point is that much of what we call fellowship, while socially delightful, is not recognizable as *koinonia*. Social activities are truly worthwhile and good for developing Christian friendships. But Jesus observed that such relationships are common in our fallen world. While they are pleasant and even necessary, they differ from the brotherly affection he calls us to. Our social connections in the church seem similar to social clubs, political caucuses, or hobby groups. Jesus calls us to something more. He calls us to *koinonia*.

The significance of *koinonia's* absence was illustrated by a situation in the early Corinthian church, where the Lord's Supper was celebrated just after a regular meal of food brought from home. Wealthy and poor Christians gathered together for worship, but during the meal that followed, the wealthy Christians enjoyed their sumptuous meals while the poor Christians managed with very little. That's not how you treat family. Paul charged that such behavior "despised the church of God" and merited a disciplinary response from God.[13] Insensitive social segregation among Christians sabotages the spiritual meaning of the Lord's Supper and makes our worship displeasing to the Lord. Acceptable worship is linked to Christian *koinonia*.

---

[12] Matthew 18:15-17; 1 John 3:14-15.
[13] 1 Corinthians 11:17-34.

The place of fellowship in Peter's Principles

Brotherly affection is unnatural and will not happen spontaneously. It must be learned. The world cannot teach us how to do this since it only knows of relationships bound together by what is mutually pleasant or advantageous and disintegrates when they cease to be so.

I learn the nature of biblical fellowship as part of the discipleship process and according to the dynamics of Peter's Principles. Brotherly affection requires me to work with the Holy Spirit to abide in Christ as he reshapes my character. Peter tells us how to make this actionable. I start by bathing in Christ's grace regularly to nurture the aspiration to find myself in him, study God's truth, make changes out of obedience, and practice those changes through trials and challenges. I then use these four steps over and over to increase my love for God by reshaping my life around who he is. As I do that—and only as I do that—I can learn to appreciate others who know the same Living God and follow Jesus, whoever they may be.

Earlier, we looked at Peter's last face-to-face conversation with Jesus before his ascension. Note how Peter's love for Christ was channeled into love for Christ's Church:

> He said to him the third time, "Simon, son of John, do you love me?" Peter was grieved because he said to him the third time, "Do you love me?" and he said to him, "Lord, you know everything; you know that I love you." Jesus said to him, "Feed my sheep." (John 21:17)

Jesus linked Peter's love for him with Peter's willingness to care for any sheep in God's flock. If we truly love the Lord, we will grow to love all his people because he loves them.

Just as I use the four character-building steps to reshape my life around God, I can begin to use them to reshape my life around his Church. With constantly refreshed aspiration and biblical understanding, I can exercise self-control to do something I've never done before that treats Christ's Church as my spiritual family and then develop steadfastness in doing that consistently over time. I can repeat this cycle over and over.

Some ideas for new obedience to develop brotherly affection: Pray for the needs of other Christians in the congregation, and teach our children to pray for them. If we don't know the people we pray for, then we get to know them. Introduce our children to the people we are praying for. Volunteer to help church seniors, young children, or single Moms—ask your Pastor for ideas. Participate in local parachurch ministries and serve with Christians outside of your own fellowship. The point is to move beyond our church friends and embrace others connected to the same Jesus. Fellowship continues to grow as we invest in Christians of other cultures, visiting nearby churches in different neighborhoods or even using a family vacation to visit churches in an area of missions activity that our church supports. I'm not focusing now on reaching unbelievers. I'm talking about getting to know Christians who are different from us but part of our extended spiritual family.

Exercising brotherly affection to address interpersonal conflict also must be learned.[14] I've found that role-playing conflicts in a group setting can be fun and effective. As in tabletop war games, you can safely investigate effective strategies when real bullets aren't flying. We can also practice treating shared Christian faith as more important than differing political opinions. Worshiping or praying with Christians on the other political side would help because that lifts up the Heavenly Father, Savior, and Holy Spirit we share, so our common love for God can create *koinonia*.

It is significant that Peter lists brotherly affection before the last step of an unrestricted love for all people. Brotherly affection helps us love people who are different but who try to love us back because we both know Christ. For love, that's like training wheels. Those wheels are finally laid aside when we

---

[14] A resource I have appreciated is *The Peacemaker*, Ken Sande, Baker Books, 2004.

reach Peter's final step: love for everyone, even when they do not love us back.

Love for God's people in the pursuit of Christ's mission.

We can only build the kingdom of God as consistently as we can genuinely love. It's that simple.

> If I speak with the tongues of men and of angels, but do not have love, I have become a noisy gong or a clanging cymbal. And if I have the gift of prophecy, and know all mysteries and all knowledge; and if I have all faith, so as to remove mountains, but do not have love, I am nothing. And if I give all my possessions to feed the poor, and if I deliver my body to be burned, but do not have love, it profits me nothing. (1 Corinthians 13:1-3)

Anything we do to extend the kingdom of God beyond ourselves requires love. *Anything.* Without love, my service for Christ "profits me nothing." Apart from my love, Christ's love is invisible. Apart from love, God's glory is not fully manifested in the world. Apart from love, the Holy Spirit's power is an unverifiable and unconvincing secondhand report. Love manifests Jesus Christ because it faithfully treats God and others as Christ sees them. My discipleship is only successful when I learn how to love as Jesus loves. Only then can I partake of the divine nature. Only then can I extend God's kingdom beyond myself.

Love must be learned, and it is learned in stages. Peter takes pains to teach that I can't effectively jump directly from faith to love for my neighbor. I *can't.* I begin by learning to love God. The many changes that loving God calls for make it look very hard, but loving God is the *easiest* kind of love I can learn. No one else is as worthy of love as he is. Forgiveness is a difficult component of love, and he is the only one I never have to forgive. He does everything he possibly can to encourage me in my efforts to love him. That's what he made me for; he wants me to learn love even more than I do. This is the place to start.

Love for God naturally motivates love for others whom he loves as much as he loves me. But loving my brethren is more challenging than loving God. They are not as easy to love as God is. In fact, they are as difficult to love as I am. The Church is where I practice loving people outside of my natural family and friendships in relationships that are subject to all the typical life conflicts. At least my spiritual family will try to love me back, which really helps. It is a great stepping stone to loving those outside the church who may not love me back.

§

Learning to love my extended Christian family is a necessary step to loving everyone, and loving everyone is essential to bring God's kingdom into the world. We may be able to put up with non-Christians who are different or hostile to us, but how do we learn to *love* them? The answer is to first learn to love Christians who are different and perhaps even hostile. Once our love is no longer corralled by social, ethnic, age, gender, or political differences and no longer afraid of conflict, it is much easier to love our neighbors.

At this point, we're ready to move to Peter's last step: love for everyone.

Discussion Questions for Chapter 11

1. What do you think it would be like to discover an entire branch of your family that you did not know existed?
2. What is *koinonia*?
   a) How is it different from natural family relationships? friendships?
   b) How would you recognize it if you saw it?
3. Have you ever seen Christian brotherly affection overcome social, racial, or political differences?
   a) How do you think the Church's impact on our culture would change if *koinonia* became common among us?
4. How is our love for each other dependent on our love for God?
   a) How is our love for our neighbor supported by our love for each other?

Chapter 12: Love

For this very reason, make every effort to supplement your faith with virtue, and virtue with knowledge, and knowledge with self-control, and self-control with steadfastness, and steadfastness with godliness, and godliness with brotherly affection, **and brotherly affection with love**. (2 Peter 1:5-7)

Suppose you wanted to point out a person who loved everyone; you would choose Jesus. You would not choose Peter—not that he was particularly stand-offish or hateful—he just wasn't any more loving than the rest of us. The New Testament gives considerable attention to his racism. That sounds strange to say to American ears because the divide between Jews and Gentiles was not as dehumanizing as chattel slavery. But the hatred between Jews and non-Jews was as great a racial divide as any in human history. The Bible chronicles Israel's Egyptian slavery, devastation by the Assyrians, humiliation at the hands of Babylon, narrow avoidance of extinction in Persia, and occupation by Rome. And that doesn't include their horrific struggle with the remnant of Alexander's empire that preceded Rome. Like all Jews, this was Peter's heritage. In Galilee, he grew up without Gentile friends or neighbors. He had never eaten Gentile food or set foot in a Gentile house and intended to keep it that way.

Jesus taught Peter to love his neighbor, any neighbor, by a series of steps. First, Jesus won over Peter's heart for God. Peter's eyes were the first to see God in Jesus the way you see a father in his son. Peter loved the mix of transcendent purpose and down-to-earth compassion that he learned about God by living with Jesus.

The next step was learning to share Jesus like a flock shares one Shepherd. Peter tasted that in Jesus' small group of 12 and the larger group of Christ's followers. Peter learned it big time on Pentecost. The list of Jews present for Peter's first sermon on Pentecost was amazingly cosmopolitan: "Parthians and Medes and Elamites and residents of Mesopotamia, Judea and Cappadocia, Pontus and Asia, Phrygia and Pamphylia, Egypt and the parts of Libya belonging to Cyrene, and visitors from Rome, both Jews and proselytes, Cretans and Arabians."[1] Three thousand of the first Christians came from this diverse group, all Jews by birth or conversion, but with different languages, local customs, politics, and points of view. Very soon, love for all Christians, regardless of ethnicity, shaped the Church's organization when Peter dealt with the conflict between Hebraic and Hellenistic Jewish widows.

But Jesus was not yet done with Peter. His last words to his apostles had been, "You will be my witnesses in Jerusalem and in all Judea and Samaria, and to the end of the earth."[2] Embracing every kind of Jew as his family in Christ had been Peter's first step, the "Jerusalem and Judea."

Samaria was next. Samaritans were a mixed race. Due to their conquest by Gentiles centuries earlier, they were only half-Jews, at best. One of the men who dealt with the widows' concerns, Philip, traveled from Judea to Samaria. He preached Christ, and many believed. As encouraging as this was, it was also a cause of concern for the Church's early leaders. Shouldn't these people dedicate themselves fully to Judaism to follow Christ? Peter was chosen to go to Samaria to see what

---

[1] Acts 2:9-11
[2] Acts 1:8.

was happening and resolve the issue.[3] When he saw the same manifestation of the Holy Spirit there that he had seen at Pentecost, he was persuaded that even half-Jews were equal members of God's kingdom family through faith in Christ. That was the "Samaria" step.

The third step changed the Church, changed Christianity, changed history, and changed Peter. All of the tenth chapter of Acts is devoted to describing it. God directly told Peter to take the gospel to a Gentile—not a half-Jew, not even a Gentile who converted to Judaism, but a Gentile who worshiped the God of the Old Testament but had never become a Jew. Peter did not want to go. Peter did not want to set foot in the man's house. But the vision God gave him was insistent, and he obeyed. The last barrier was shattered when Peter saw the same manifestation of the Holy Spirit in Cornelius's house that he had seen at Pentecost and in Samaria.

The first great council of the Church was convened to decide whether Gentiles had to first become Jews in order to become Christians.[4] Paul put forth the radical notion that since salvation was by faith alone, Gentiles should be accepted as equal brothers and sisters in Christ with no need to convert to Judaism. However, it was Peter's speech that won hearts and minds, resulting in the Council's historic decision. Peter would continue to struggle with his prejudices.[5] In the end, however, he embraced Christ's mission to the nations, accepting Gentile believers as equal members of his spiritual family. Now, the gospel was on its way to every nation.

Simon was the first to see Jesus as Daniel's Son of Man from heaven.[6] From then on, not even the Gates of Hell could stop worldwide kingdom growth. Simon's nickname testified to his key role. As Daniel's ever-expanding *rock*, Peter was chosen to introduce the gospel to all the Jews (Jerusalem and Judea), to Samaria, and, by including Gentiles as equal

---

[3] Acts 8:4-17.

[4] Acts 15.

[5] Galatians 2:11-14.

[6] The meaning of this is explained in Chapter 1.

partners, "to the end of the earth." God's kingdom burst forth from Israel through Peter to circle the globe.

The offer of the gospel to everyone, to every neighbor in the world, changed evangelism. For two thousand years, the good news had been of God's faithful covenant with the children of Abraham and those Gentiles who joined them. Israel had been the vessel, the prototype kingdom whose purpose was fulfilled in Jesus. From then on, God's larger promise to Abraham would be fulfilled, and "all the families of the earth will be blessed"—blessed directly through faith to create one family of God in Christ.[7]

Now, the message of salvation needed to be concisely explained to Gentiles, and the good works that freely go with gospel witness had to be adapted to each culture. Peter learned to care for everyone and offer Christ to everyone regardless of their response.

Thus, a man who grew up in the cultural backwater of Galilee with all the ethnic prejudices of his day was transformed by Jesus Christ. He spent the rest of his life loving people of all kinds, races, nations, cultures, and backgrounds from Jerusalem to Rome, regardless of whether they responded with faith or lethal hatred. Simon had indeed become Peter, the one chosen to initiate the expansion of God's kingdom to everyone, everywhere.

§

Discipleship equips me to discover my identity in the character and love of Christ. As I grasp the flow from faith through aspiration, knowledge, obedience, and steadfastness, I wrap my character around Christ. His character in me can then bring love to my relationships. I begin by learning to love God. As I grow in love for God, his love for all his spiritual children changes my relationship with them. My love stretches beyond my natural family and friends as I treat other

---

[7] Genesis 12:1-3; Romans 4; Galatians 3:7-9.

Christians—all of them—as my spiritual family. Ultimately, as I grow in mutual love with Christians who are different from me, I am prepared to love *anyone,* and I can begin to find my place in Christ's mission.

The last of Peter's steps is translated simply as *love* and is not limited to fellow believers. It isn't limited at all. All three of Peter's last steps of discipleship involve love, but only the last one uses the particular word that uniquely came to describe love in the Christian faith. The Greek word *agape* used to be translated in English as "charity" to distinguish it from the mutual, two-way love we are used to. That's because *agape* is different. *Agape* is one-way love, a manifestation of Christian character flowing from the inside out.

One-way love

Once, when a teacher asked Jesus how to inherit eternal life, Jesus asked the man what he thought. The teacher summarized the law of God, saying that we must love God above all and our neighbors as ourselves. Jesus agreed that if that man could love everyone perfectly, he would earn God's blessing. The teacher quickly realized that he had acknowledged a higher standard that he could reach and turned the conversation to how he might limit "neighbor" to people he was prepared to love.

Jesus responded with his famous parable about a man robbed and left for dead by the side of the road.[8] Religious Jews walked by, pretending not to notice. Only a Samaritan, from an ethnic group despised by Jews, stopped and gave generous love to this needy stranger. Jesus completely turned the teacher's question on its head. Instead of answering who our neighbors are, Jesus asked which person in the parable *was* a neighbor to the stricken man. Sinners limit love to preferred relationships. For Christ, love is a matter of character, not preference. Love depends on who we are rather than who the other person is.

---

[8] Luke 10:25-37.

The parable of the Good Samaritan expresses how Jesus viewed the love he came to give and to inspire among his followers. Of course, it is natural for love to express goodwill toward members of our preferred groups, who typically love us in return. That is all fine and good. But Christ's love, God's love, *agape* love, flows from character and is manifested in every relationship. It is not called forth by someone else's group identity, virtues, or response to us. Instead, Christ's love overflows from the virtue inside us and is given to anyone.

This is the love that characterizes the God of the Bible, who

- generously created humanity to share his joy in all he made.[9]
- freely promised Abraham his blessing, even at the cost of God's own life.[10]
- made Israel his treasure before they were given his law.[11]
- promised David a dynasty he did not deserve.[12]
- promised redemption to a people who often failed him.[13]
- ultimately sent the Son he loves to redeem sinners.[14]

Agape loves as God loves, as Christ loves. Because it flows from God's divine character in us, it does not depend on whether others deserve it or return it. *Agape* is one-way love.

The Uniqueness of Christ's love

In some ways, the love of Christ is like any other genuine love, whether for parents, spouses, children, close friends, one's country, or an animal companion. In each case, you

---

[9] Genesis 1-2.
[10] Genesis 15:7-21.
[11] Exodus 20:1-2.
[12] 2 Samuel 7:1-17.
[13] Jeremiah 31.
[14] John 3:16-17; Titus 3:1-7.

identify so closely with the loved ones that you are emotionally moved to self-sacrifice. You don't have to follow Christ to truly love someone and even give your life for them. Anyone can recognize real love when they see it. It is beautiful. It is uplifting and often inspiring.

> Love is patient and kind; love does not envy or boast; it is not arrogant or rude. It does not insist on its own way; it is not irritable or resentful; it does not rejoice at wrongdoing, but rejoices with the truth. Love bears all things, believes, hopes, and endures all things. Love never ends. (1 Corinthians 13:4-8)

Non-Christians genuinely appreciate 1 Corinthians 13 and enjoy quoting it. What is unique about Christ's love is *who* he loves:

> For while we were still weak, at the right time Christ died for the ungodly. For one will scarcely die for a righteous person —though perhaps for a good person one would dare even to die— but God shows his love for us in that while we were still sinners, Christ died for us. (Romans 5:6-8)

God's love is related to his redemption, but they are distinct. God's redemption is his saving work of sovereign grace that is always echoed by a free response of faith. But God's love is his goodwill that freely streams to all, like the sunshine and rain, regardless of response. His goodwill gives everyone natural life. His goodwill offers everlasting life to whoever believes in his Son. Christ's love welcomes and never casts away any who come to him.[15]

Agape is not the only kind of genuine love. Jesus had a family who was special to him. Jesus cultivated a mutual love with disciples whom he called friends. But in terms of unswerving goodwill, Jesus loved everyone—followers and enemies, humble and proud, obnoxious sinners and morally blind sinners. Everyone. Even today, no one ever has to earn

---

[15] John 6:37.

Jesus' love. It emerges from his inner character as naturally as a vine produces grapes. Fallen human love depends on the quality of selected relationships. *Agape* does not. *Agape* is genuine, practical goodwill toward all.

Christ calls his followers to love like him and, therefore, to love like God. The outworking of that goodwill takes many forms depending on the situation and opportunity. *Agape* does not always do what others want but always serves according to need. It is gentle and patient, even when it must be firm. It allows the freedom to run from God but burns no bridges in case there is a change of heart. It is never a thin veneer of niceness but cares deeply about spiritual and material well-being. While it is universal, it is also particular to each person, not a checklist of mere duties but welcome opportunities to do the same good I would wish to have done for me if situations were reversed. It is honest goodwill toward everyone.

My Story

Early on, my journey to love everyone had to face my remarkable naivety about racism. I grew up in the thoroughly segregated Maryland of the 1950s. My exposure to African Americans came through old Tarzan movies, the television version of *Amos and Andy*, and the occasional sympathetic appearance of formerly enslaved people on prime-time Westerns. That limited exposure was incredible, considering I grew up *one block* from a Black neighborhood. It might as well have been a continent away. I have no memory of seeing a Black person in school, church (my grandmother took me when I was very young), or any store or movie theater. The 1950 census of my hometown of Annapolis says that over 36% of the population was non-White, but for me, they were virtually invisible. My family never spoke of them disparagingly. My family never spoke of them at all. As formal segregation was lifted and I began going to school with Blacks, I wondered where they all had suddenly come from!

Throughout the '60s, I watched the Civil Rights movement on TV, wondering what all the commotion was about. Slavery was obviously wrong, and it all happened so long ago. Why couldn't Whites and Blacks in the South get along? I had no idea what this hatred was about or that it was not restricted to the South.

My college experience was integrated, and I can't remember any discomfort with that, although all my friends were White. I didn't realize anything was amiss until my days in seminary. For a time, I led a co-ed community of Christian students saving money by renting a house together. One was an African American I'll call Henry. Henry attended Harvard (our house was just a few blocks from Harvard Yard). He was as good a man as any I knew. But one day, I was shocked to feel like I should wash my palm after shaking hands with him as if his blackness might rub off on me.

I was stunned. Though I had not realized it before, something in me instinctively thought Blacks were dirty. In the following years, I struggled to understand the Black American experience, though I had little guidance, and my progress was slow. I had no negative feelings toward Blacks that I could discern, but there was no denying that they felt foreign to me, and I could not love them as I loved myself.

I tried several times to jump-start my love for African Americans. One summer, I volunteered in Washington, D.C., teaching Black children in a vacation Bible school. I felt utterly ineffective. Then I spent an entire summer living in inner-city Philadelphia as part of an evangelism project. The only fruit I saw that summer came from incidental influence in a suburban White congregation. At some point, I just gave up, assuming that I would never understand or relate to this significant segment of Americans.

Then, years later, I visited a Black pastor of inner-city Baltimore in his home and shared an afternoon as he walked the streets greeting his neighbors. I don't think I've ever seen a church more involved in sharing the gospel and making good things happen for its surrounding community. I could relate to this brother and admired his spirit.

Suddenly, I realized what I lacked in my discipleship. I had learned how to grow in my love for my Lord, and the Holy Spirit built on that to help me love God's people. But the only people of God I knew were White. I could leverage my love for all sorts of White Christians to care for all kinds of White non-Christians. But to develop a functioning love for Black people in general, I needed first to cultivate a love for Black Christians, bridging cultural distance as we tried to love each other. Leveraging those relationships would be the key to forging a love for all Black Americans regardless of their attitude toward me.

I mentioned that Black Americans were foreign to me, but the truth is that everybody outside of my experience is foreign to me—people from Asia, the Middle East and India, Native Americans, and Latins. Also, people who are desperately poor, forcibly removed from their homes, suffering catastrophic health problems, fleeing for their lives from their native country, billionaires, celebrities, people living in the inner city, farmers, high government officials, professional athletes, and many others whose life experience is different from mine. For me, the key to one-way love is to first learn to love Christians like them. Then, when my experience of *koinonia* removes the otherness and foreignness of our differences, I am much better prepared to love similar non-Christians. I only wish I had realized this five decades ago. This should be part of the training of any disciple of Jesus, just as it had been for Peter.

The place of *agape* love in Peter's Principles

Developing a character that naturally reproduces Christ's one-way love for everyone is the ultimate goal of discipleship. It is a partaking of the divine nature. We must not let our inability to attain perfection obscure our potential to develop this kind of love. Peter says it is not only possible to develop it but impossible not to if we abide in Christ. *Agape* love is not supposed to be rare. Over the last two thousand years, it has been the most authentic mark of following Christ.

Agape is the last of Peter's steps. In one sense, all the steps are equally important because they are all necessary. But in another sense, *agape* is the most important because, without it, all the other elements fail to attain discipleship's goal. If a staircase has seven steps, what good is it to climb only six?

Partaking of the divine nature means sharing God's goodwill toward every human being. This is not just an admirable goal. It is not a spiritual extra. Since it is the expression of Christ's character applied to relationships, it is what human beings were made for—what I was made for—and learning how to pursue it effectively is the goal of discipleship.

I must repeatedly stress this point. We have not effectively been discipled, and we have not effectively discipled someone else simply by leading a group study of prepared material (like this book, for example). Such studies are a tool. But discipleship is only accomplished when it prepares us for a journey to love people as Christ loves them. That does not mean our discipleship enables us to love quickly or perfectly. Spiritual growth is a life-long process. Discipleship is initial training in how to grow in our love. I will retrace the steps of Peter's Principles thousands of times but will not complete them even once until I love one neighbor who is unlike me, as Jesus does. This change will glorify God, bring me joy, invigorate the Church, and empower my witness.

Agape love in the pursuit of Christ's mission

All of Peter's previous steps deal with teaching existing disciples how to live in the kingdom of God together. The last step involves us with everyone currently outside of the kingdom. *Agape* can be manifested in two ways, as suggested in one of Jesus' illustrations:

> Enter by the narrow gate. For the gate is wide and the way is easy that leads to destruction, and those who enter by it are many. For the gate is narrow and the way is hard that leads to life, and those who find it are few. (Matthew 7:13-14)

Agape love manifests the narrow way through *good works* and points to the narrow gate through *evangelism*.

Good works

Agape love empowers good works, a label for everything we do that benefits others regardless of who they are. Doing good was Peter's first theme as he introduced Jesus to the Gentile Cornelius:

> God anointed Jesus of Nazareth with the Holy Spirit and with power. He went about doing good and healing all who were oppressed by the devil, for God was with him. (Acts 10:38)

Good works are the natural outcome of following Jesus. Jesus continues to do good through the Holy Spirit, only now his Church serves as his Body on earth.[16] Three times in his two letters, Peter encourages all Christians to "do good."[17] Twice, the Apostle Paul urged believers not to grow weary in doing good,[18] and after he reviewed salvation by grace in his letter to Titus, he went on to say,

> I want you to insist on these things, so that those who have believed in God may be careful to devote themselves to good works. These things are excellent and profitable for people. (Titus 3:8)

The term "good works" has an archaic feel to it. The core idea involves the expenditure of energy (the underlying Greek word gives us the modern term "energy"). We do good works when we expend energy to do something worthwhile and helpful for others. Think of it as making good things happen for people, understanding good things as those which provide real benefit.

The Apostle Paul's most well-known connection between salvation by grace and our good works is in the Book of Ephesians,

> For by grace you have been saved through faith. And this is not your own doing; it is the gift of God, not a result of works, so that no one may boast. For we are his

---

[16] 1 Corinthians 12.

[17] 1 Peter 2:15; 3:17; 4:19.

[18] Galatians 6:9; 2 Thessalonians 3:13.

workmanship, created in Christ Jesus for good works, which God prepared beforehand, that we should walk in them. (Ephesians 2:8-10)

Salvation by grace is at the heart of Jesus' one-way love that gives out of his inner character rather than because of some virtue in us or benefit from us. The New Testament expects faithful Christians to manifest the same one-way love by making good things happen for others—not only for Christians or others we are naturally attracted to but for everyone. The good works the apostles spoke of are motivated by inner character and do not depend on the recipient's faith or response.

Good works are pursued within our cultural roles: family, career, church, and surrounding community. We typically view such roles in terms of self-fulfillment or self-expression and tend to do good things that return responses beneficial to us. That is not necessarily bad, but it is not *agape*. *Agape* love seeks to benefit others simply according to need, often anonymously as a self-check to ensure we don't do it mostly for thanks or reward.[19]

Good works are not unwanted duties done under pressure. They are never for show. Christians love their neighbors on this planet in thoughtful and practical ways simply because it is the nature of Christ's love to do so. Thanks are certainly appreciated, and new faith is always celebrated, but good works stand on their own as genuine, heartfelt, one-way love. *Agape* is a character quality and a matter of integrity. It needs no more compensation from others than telling the truth or being fair. Good works are simply what growing Christian disciples want to do.

Following Jesus' example, good works usually take the form of meeting needs. Just because we cannot solve all the problems of our world, church, workplace, or family doesn't mean we can't help. We can often do something in response to needs, from practical aid to drawing attention to a problem to

---

[19] Matthew 6:2-4.

humble offers of comfort and understanding. There are all kinds of financial and emotional needs, along with health concerns and the crush of circumstances. Christians learning to love like Jesus will not turn away from any of them. When we hear of suffering, we look to God with sadness, lift those who suffer to him and help if we can. We can do this even in response to the unending procession of tragedy we call the daily news. We must not look away. We will not become overwhelmed if we remember we are not given the burden of fixing the world. We help where we can simply because we can. In doing so, we demonstrate the conviction that the good we do is a foretaste of what Jesus will accomplish when he returns to make all things right and new.

We cannot do every good work. Over time, *agape* develops practiced responses that suit our convictions, insight, resources, and opportunity. We might support lonely neighbors, operate food banks, write books, send letters of encouragement, teach English as a second language, produce art that exposes need or stimulates joy, or sponsor worthy community projects. Sometimes we can individually make good things happen for others, and sometimes we can do it as part of Church efforts. Sometimes we can do good works in concert with caring non-Christians. Every instance of one-way love becomes an occasion for joy and satisfaction because we manifest Jesus' goodwill.

One way to think of a Christian's approach to politics is to see it as a form of good works. We do not blindly serve an ideology or party. Instead, we work for Christ to make good things happen for fellow citizens and do it the best way we know how. We work with non-Christians when our interests overlap, bringing the gospel to bear wherever possible. In politics, as in everywhere else, we do good works because it is a disciple's nature and desire to do so, regardless of whether or not we accumulate power or receive gratitude and fame. Christ will express divine good pleasure in our efforts when he returns, which is more than enough.

Ultimately, good works embrace every aspect of the Cultural Mandate. It describes all our efforts to make the world a better place for everyone to live. Good works spend energy to express compassion, mercy, righteousness, and justice. Discipleship should prepare us to pursue good works in every role and area of life.

Another powerful manifestation of *agape* is goodwill toward people who have wronged us or who have become our enemies for any reason.

> You have heard that it was said, "You shall love your neighbor and hate your enemy." But I say to you, love your enemies and pray for those who persecute you, so that you may be sons of your Father who is in heaven. For he makes his sun rise on evil and good, and sends rain on the just and the unjust. (Matthew 5:43-45)

The reference to God's provision for all mankind implies that the goodwill Jesus has in mind is not limited to fellow believers. As is so characteristic of *agape*, there are no limits to Christian goodwill. Note that *agape* does not, by itself, create or require reconciliation. Reconciliation is wonderful, but it is a two-way effort and involves repentance from sin. *Agape* is a character trait that brings one-way goodwill into any relationship, regardless of whether the ones who hurt us repent. We desire reconciliation, but goodwill does not depend on relationships being healed. Discipleship should prepare us to love those who hurt us.

Good works and goodwill toward everyone are what life in the kingdom of God looks like. They are the fruit that grows from abiding in Christ. Peter tells us that such fruit does not grow magically from the root of faith without connecting vines and branches, which are the seven qualities discipleship should introduce to the believer.

If others are attracted to the narrow way they see Christians taking, how can they find the narrow gate to enter it?

Evangelism

Evangelism communicates the gospel to everyone, identifying Jesus as the gate into the kingdom of God that

Christians make visible in how we live. I discussed the content of the gospel—how Christ opened that door—in the earlier chapter on Faith.

The gospel is for all people. Therefore, evangelism is another aspect of *agape* or one-way love. As we have seen, *agape* love does not appear magically out of faith. It is an outgrowth of love for God's diverse people, which is itself an outgrowth of love for God, which is a product of character development, which must be ever-resting on God's abundant grace. When we engage in evangelism that is not an outgrowth of our love for God's diverse people, it tends to keep people who aren't like us at arm's length. When we engage in evangelism that is not an outgrowth of our love for God, it tends to be self-exalting and spiritually hollow. When we engage in evangelism that is not an outgrowth of inner character, evangelism becomes manipulative. When we engage in evangelism that is not an outgrowth of God's grace, we don't communicate the true gospel.

Christ's mission pairs evangelism with good works/goodwill to expand the kingdom of God. Either one without the other is good, but Jesus wants them together. Jesus typically provided good works and goodwill first and then proclaimed the good news, thus first demonstrating and then explaining the kingdom.

Good works and goodwill develop first within the Church's brotherly affection because it is the nature of families to care for each other.[20] Christians demonstrate God's power within us when we make good things happen in the lives of Christians beyond our natural circle of relationships and despite interpersonal conflict.

The *koinonia* observed within the Church empowers *agape* evangelism outside the Church. Consider how Luke points this out in the Book of Acts in the way Acts 2:47 flows out of verses 42-46 and Acts 6:7 flows out of verses 1-6. I am particularly drawn to an example in Acts 4:

---

[20] Galatians 6:10.

> Now the full number of those who believed were of one
> heart and soul, and no one said that any of the things that
> belonged to him was his own, but they had everything in
> common. And with great power the apostles were giving
> their testimony to the resurrection of the Lord Jesus, and
> great grace was upon them all. (Acts 4:32-33)

Luke implies that the transformation of unrelated Christians to practically love each other supplied evidence to the apostles' testimony of Christ's resurrection. Any idol can support an artificial religion. But Christian strangers became part of a family-style partnership that only made sense if they all knew Jesus, implying that he truly rose from the dead. Visible good works and healed relationships within the Church are potent testimonies that Jesus is alive, risen, and Lord of all.

Good works and goodwill extend beyond the Church,[21] not as a technique to win approval or entice people to faith but as a direct result of what Christians have become. Christians do good works and display goodwill out of *agape* love because people who follow Jesus become like him. *Agape* helps anyone, anytime, to the limit of our ability, wisdom, and opportunity, even those who consider themselves our enemies. Good works and goodwill demonstrate the truth of the gospel.

It is not wise to heavily promote gospel sharing apart from goodwill and good works. It's fine to have a summary of the gospel ready for strangers during the 30 seconds it takes for a plane to crash. There is no reason, however, to limit the sharing of Christ to a few verbal formulas when there are Christians nearby who could provide living evidence of Christ's resurrection. The point is not that evangelism cannot stand on its own. The point is how outreach is meant to work. Jesus explicitly stated that unity inspired by *agape* love identifies his followers and provides evidence that the world needs to see that the gospel is true.[22] Why can't we believe

---

[21] 1 Thessalonians 5:15.

[22] John 15:8;17:20-23.

him? Evangelism points to the gate, but people must want what is on the other side before they go through it.

When speaking of conversion, it's tempting to reference the mysterious ways the Holy Spirit draws people, but what if his ways aren't so mysterious? What if the Holy Spirit enables faith through the observable evidence of people who love God, love each other, and love everyone because they are followers of the risen Lord Jesus Christ?

The one-way love that shares the gospel in the context of good works and goodwill can be costly. But the hard part about Christ's mission is not this cost because *agape* love sacrifices willingly. The hard part about Christ's mission is developing the character, love for God, and love for God's people that make love for everyone possible. When I try to step up to *agape* love directly from saving faith, I fail and start trusting ministry techniques to make evangelism successful. But techniques do not create love, and without love, even proclaiming God's truth amounts to nothing.[23] Character and love were how Jesus prepared Peter. That's what discipleship is for.

The good news is that when we make every effort to allow each of Peter's qualities overflow to the next, good works and evangelism are absolutely guaranteed. We will always find ways to accomplish those things because we will have found our new identity in Christ's love.

§

This completes our brief overview of Peter's seven steps of discipleship. I invite the reader to expand on each step with insights accumulated over a lifetime. All that is left is to draw some conclusions and applications.

---

[23] 1 Corinthians 13:2.

Discussion Questions for Chapter 12

1. Share a natural example of love that you've seen outside of a faith context that moved you deeply.
2. What is the difference between Christ's love and the love people naturally experience?
   a) How does the parable of the Good Samaritan demonstrate love?
3. How does love for people who are unlike us in Christ's Church prepare us to love everyone?
4. What does it mean to love people who hurt us?
5. Discuss one-way love in relation to Christ's mission.
   a) Make a list of good works that contribute to the Cultural Mandate.
   b) What would make evangelism truly an expression of *agape* love?
   c) Discuss the interplay of good works/goodwill and evangelism.

Conclusions

2 Peter 1:11-15

Chapter 13: Your Story

For whoever lacks these qualities is so nearsighted that he is blind, having forgotten that he was cleansed from his former sins. Therefore, brothers, be all the more diligent to confirm your calling and election, for if you practice these qualities you will never fall. For in this way there will be richly provided for you an entrance into the eternal kingdom of our Lord and Savior Jesus Christ. (2 Peter 1:9-11)

Christians reading through Peter's seven-step reflection upon his discipleship will naturally compare this to their own experience. I certainly did. So I'm glad Peter addressed those of us whose discipleship experience was incomplete.

What if I am spiritually stuck? What if I've been stuck for a long time? For those of us who have never been fully trained to follow Jesus as Peter was or who have been but are out of practice, Peter generously remarks that we are *nearsighted*. To be nearsighted is to see only things near, right in front of our faces. The background is blurry.

Studies have shown that too much screen time contributes to myopia or nearsightedness. What an appropriate illustration of the unregulated impact of our online culture. I become spiritually nearsighted when focusing too long on the values and opinions society puts in my face. I may believe God is real and rules over all, but he is in the background and becomes blurry. Peter says believers can get so nearsighted that they become blind to God. We can no longer see him, not in the world, not in others, not in what is happening to us, and not in what is happening inside us. He is still there, but he's a blur.

Peter understands. He remembers losing sight of Christ when the whole world plunged into darkness. But Peter later discovered what we might forget when wandering in the dark. Jesus has not lost sight of his flock and never stops loving us. Peter was reminded that he was not originally chosen after a job interview or an analysis of his potential. Jesus simply called him and promised the power to follow. He called us the same way, but perhaps we don't see that so clearly.

If you are concerned that the problem is more than nearsightedness—if you are unsure that Christ has called you and you are part of his kingdom—then start over. If you were never saved, it's time for Jesus to save you right now. First, make sure you want to follow Jesus:

- because of his life that you recognize as God's design for all of us, and for you in particular
- his sacrificial death to deal with every failure you have made or will ever make
- his resurrection that powers a new life you can share with him
- his leadership that deserves your pledge to follow him from now on
- his promised return from Heaven to make all things new forever.

Declare to God your desire to follow Jesus. He will hear you; he has been waiting for this moment for a long time and is rejoicing more than you can imagine.[1] Then confess it within Christ's Church by embracing the outward sign of discipleship either by asking to be baptized in your church or, if you are already baptized, thoughtfully reaffirming what your church asks believers to confess when they are baptized. If you don't

---

[1] Zephaniah 3:17; Luke 15:3-7.

have a church, ask for recommendations from a Christian you know and respect. Look for a church that uses the Bible as God's Word and has people who remind you of Jesus.

And if you already have faith but realize that you've been dozing, then rejoice that you are waking up![2]

Then what? How do I keep my spiritual eyesight from becoming blurry in the future? Peter says, "If you practice these qualities you will never fall." Approach your calling to follow Jesus with fresh enthusiasm. Practice moving through each of Peter's first four steps and find ways to adapt your lifestyle within the relationships highlighted in the final three steps. Ask your church for someone to provide direction and encouragement. You may find that others would like to join you on the journey.

The story of the new you

This journey builds upon your faith in what Christ has done for you and has already done in you. Your faith demonstrates that at the core of your being, you have been reborn.[3] Think about that. Being reborn is not just about the moment of rebirth. It is about the beginning of a new life. Underneath layer upon layer of sin—dead layers of brokenness, half-truths, and complete lies—the Holy Spirit has brought the core of your being alive to God. At birth, a baby doesn't know anything but that he or she is alive. An infant does not know how to think, feel or behave. The same is true of spiritual rebirth. We know we are alive to God but understand very little about how to think, feel or behave as God's child. The difference between birth and rebirth is that we face many pre-existing habits when we are spiritually reborn. Living your new life requires unlearning what has already shaped you as you wrap yourself around Jesus' character and love.

But remember: if we attempt to change our thoughts, emotions, and lifestyle by sheer willpower, we will fail. That

---

[2] Ephesians 5:8-14.
[3] John 3:1-15; 1 Peter 1:3-5.

approach treats Christ-likeness as something still alien that we're trying to force upon ourselves. Discipleship works when you build upon faith that God has awakened your heart. Down deep, underneath your life's pain and disorder, you want to follow Jesus. That faith assumes God is already working in you and draws on his strength. Faith that Jesus has already given you a reborn heart is critical to your discipleship. You are not trying to become someone else. Instead, you are freeing your reborn soul to be the person God had in mind before he made the world. You believe you have a new heart that expresses itself in Christ-likeness when given a chance, and you're open to going wherever that leads. When you feel the old attractions of greed, selfishness, lust, and pride, you know that their deep roots in your soul are disintegrating. Discipleship trains you to cooperate with a transformation powered by God and has already begun.

> ... you have heard about him and were taught in him, as the truth is in Jesus, to put off your old self, which belongs to your former manner of life and is corrupt through deceitful desires, and to be renewed in the spirit of your minds, and to put on the new self, created after the likeness of God in true righteousness and holiness. (Ephesians 4:21-24)

Christians don't have to change who they are to become like Jesus. We have already become like him in our innermost being. Our challenge is to throw off old habits, so we can live as the people we now are.

A blueprint for witness

Consider how Peter's concise guide encapsulates his story spread through the Gospels, Acts, and Epistles. Just as architects work with blueprints to aid construction, you could use Peter's Principles as a blueprint to construct your story. Evangelical tradition associates Christian witness with the story of how I came to faith in Jesus. That was the beginning of Peter's story in the Gospels, too. But Peter's story went on, and 2 Peter 1:5-7 summarizes his experience in seven steps built on saving faith, each one part of his journey with Christ.

What is the story of your journey with Christ? Once you understand and consciously experience moving from one of the seven qualities to the next, you can make that experience part of your story and witness. If you can't remember one breakthrough event that initially marked a particular transition, that's OK. You can pick any example. After all, going through Peter's Principles for the first time is basic training for the rest of your life. You will accumulate many stories along the way. Just choose one for each step.

Eventually, you will have a collection of personal experiences with Christ that describe your journey with him. Of course, sharing how you came to Christ is great when talking to someone about coming to Christ. But having a story for each of Peter's steps naturally brings your witness into a variety of conversations. It makes your witness something other than a religious debate. It's what a witness to Christ's resurrection is supposed to be: your personal experience with the risen and living Jesus. Your stories could include

- How Jesus found you; how you came to believe (faith).
- A vivid memory of how you were inspired to dedicate your life to him (virtue).
- A powerful insight from the Bible that changed your perspective (knowledge).
- An example of how your life expanded when you initiated, ended, or changed something because Jesus asked you to (self-control).
- A way that Jesus made you a better person through adversity or practice (steadfastness).
- How your friendship with God has grown through one of his biblical roles (godliness).
- An experience demonstrating you are part of a larger spiritual family (brotherly affection).
- A way that you work alongside Jesus to care for the needs of people unlike you (*agape* love).

Perhaps no stories come to your mind for one or more steps of Peter's blueprint. No problem. It would be great if we were thoroughly discipled at the beginning of our faith, but that rarely happens. Jesus is ready today through the Holy Spirit to complete your apprenticeship in how to pursue his character and love. And if you identify one particularly troublesome step, don't forget to check for blockage upstream in previous steps. Don't try to force growth with a crowbar; instead, cultivate it like a plant. Just do whatever you need to do to sustain the flow of God's life, from saving faith to one-way love.

§

If these ideas seem overwhelming, then you are precisely the Christian to whom Peter was writing. He knew we would become nearsighted and focus only on what the world holds to our faces. He knew that many would genuinely embrace the gospel, which is the power of God for salvation, yet not understand how that power works. That's why he summarized how the Holy Spirit transforms us as naturally as a branch bears fruit when we work on seven qualities related to each other in a specific way. We can learn this because it is why the Holy Spirit was sent.

You might find it helpful and encouraging to write a journal of your walk through Peter's Principles, documenting how Jesus teaches you to discover who God designed you to be. That's what Peter did in the New Testament.

I know that yours will be a story worth sharing, too.

Discussion Questions for Chapter 13

1. If you are comfortable, briefly share the beginning of your spiritual journey: How did you come to know Jesus, or what moved you to start searching?
2. Discuss Peter's use of the image of being nearsighted.
   a) How do his steps eliminate spiritual nearsightedness?
3. For how many of Peter's qualities are you able to share a story that illustrates it from your experience?
   a) To document your discipleship and fill out your witness, would you like to complete your set of stories?
   b) How might we help each other do that?

Chapter 14: Peter's Principles and the Great Commission

For we did not follow cleverly devised myths when we made known to you the power and coming of our Lord Jesus Christ, but we were eyewitnesses of his majesty. (2 Peter 1:16)

In the Introduction, I said, "The search for one's authentic self is the quest of the 21st century." The notion that we define who and what we are supposed to be is one of the cleverly devised myths we currently face. Peter addressed such myths by making the coming of Jesus Christ known and giving credence to the gospel with his personal witness that Jesus is alive. Let me apply Peter's Principles to suggest how today, our witness might enable people to reject contemporary myths and find their authentic selves in Christ.

Identity confusion

America has become so polarized that the future of our democracy is uncertain. The nation is disintegrating into two extreme camps of mutual disgust and hatred. The most turbulence is felt in politics, particularly what is described as "identity politics." Identity politics strive to overturn oppression against specific minority groups. A central strategy is to change how society officially characterizes those groups.

The groups in question recast their distinctiveness in favorable terms and press very hard for freedom to live openly as their *authentic selves.*[1] Identity politics was first associated with African Americans courageously dedicated to ridding America of its racist heritage of slavery.

More recently, however, the identity factors involved are not objective ones, like race, but are constructs of one's mind and feelings. That is, instead of seeking to live authentically as the people we objectively are, the new demand is for society to affirm the right for us to define who we are. The political battle centers on gender self-definition. It has reached the point where a Supreme Court Justice cannot explain what a woman is, and my latest medical form asked for no gender identification except whether or not I could get pregnant.

The challenge, however, is much broader. While the language of identity is most explicitly used in the LGBTQIA community and more generally on the Left side of the political spectrum, obsession with an identity we create for ourselves can describe both Left and Right. This happens when there is a preference for cultural dogma rather than objective truth and a sense of entitlement that insists if I want to live in a certain way, the government should protect and even enforce my preference. Identity politics justifies behavior and demands entitlements to preserve a group's identity and advance its agenda. To disagree with that agenda is received as a malicious assault against the group. That is a feeling shared by gay activists and White nationalists. This turns differing opinions about lifestyle into vicious cultural battles that make civil conversations difficult or impossible.

I review all this because anything that shuts down civil interaction hinders the gospel. Evangelism expresses *agape* one-way love, but it is hard to communicate love when politics hijack the conversation. Discussions of the gospel may be

---

[1] This kind of thinking is the product of long-developing trends. An excellent overview is *The Rise and Triumph of the Modern Self: Cultural Amnesia, Expressive Individualism, and the Road to Sexual Revolution,* Carl Truman, Crossway, 2020.

short-circuited or re-routed to attack or defend a lifestyle choice involving sex, the environment, race, or another divisive issue. Sometimes, behaviors the Bible identifies as sinful become the focus and are justified with a passionate appeal to one's sense of self. "That's simply who I am." We must understand that such remarks are sincere and may echo a sad history of painful experiences. But since our culture insists that this reasoning is unassailable, it ends a gospel discussion before Christ can become part of it.

Peter's Principles suggest a way forward that, along the way, recovers an evangelistic approach used by the Apostles.

Original approaches to the gospel

The early Church followed different strategies in reaching Jews versus Gentiles—people who believed in a Creator God who has revealed his character versus people who have always created their own gods. Initially, Peter was most comfortable reaching Jews, while Paul was predisposed to reach Gentiles (although, as we have seen, Peter learned over time how to reach Gentiles, as well).[2] The strategy was that to Jews, the gospel would be preached in the context of God's Old Testament revelation, promises, and law. Jesus would be proclaimed as the promised Messiah who came to fulfill the Old Testament.

The strategy to reach Gentiles was different. Typically, they were not familiar with the Old Testament. It made little sense to urge faith in promises or repentance from commandments they did not know. Instead, they introduced the gospel to Gentiles by proclaiming a Creator of the human race who deserves our worship, has the right to define the purpose and nature of our lives, and has revealed himself in Jesus Christ. For example, consider the Apostle Paul's evangelism in the Gentile town of Lystra.[3] After demonstrating Jesus' powerful

---

[2] Consider Paul's interaction with Peter and the other Apostles recorded in Galatians 2:1-10, and the work of the Jerusalem Council recorded in Acts 15.

[3] Acts 14:8-18.

compassion, he proclaimed that all humans are creatures God has made, and we should be grateful and respectful toward him in response. The initial point of his proclamation was that a Living God created and sustains us, and we should treat him accordingly. More of the gospel would be explained as people showed interest, but this is where he started.

In Athens, Paul again began with human identity.[4] He declared that all people are creatures God has made, and we should be grateful and respectful toward him in response. He discussed the significance of mankind, even quoting secular poetry to find points of contact since everyone is interested in what it means to be human. Pointing to the many Athenian idols, Paul declared that it's wrong to pretend to create our own gods and then use them to define how we want to live. He reported that the Living Creator God has revealed himself through someone who defines right and wrong for us all. Other than the fundamental sin of idolatry, Paul did not debate any of the well-known sinful behaviors in Athens. He would review those things later with those interested in exploring Jesus, but debating specific sins was not what he led with. Paul's first concern was not getting Athenians to stop stealing, hating their parents, or living as homosexuals. Paul's first concern was to declare that Jesus is bringing God's kingdom rule into the world. If Jesus captured their hearts as the Son of God, Paul could then more thoroughly discuss sin, forgiveness, and the implications of following Christ.

Paul carefully laid out this approach to the gospel in the Book of Romans. In Chapters 1-3, he began by discussing how the human race does not embrace what it was created to be. That laid a foundation on which he could then illustrate specific sins and go on to explain the nature of judgment and redemption.

As with Jews and Gentiles in the early Church, sharing the gospel could begin in different places today, depending on who we are talking to. To churched people who need Christ, we could meaningfully discuss biblical sins, promises, and

---

[4] Acts 17:16-34.

explanations of redemption. However, we need to move back several paces with the unchurched and first discuss matters of identity, the reality of the Living God, and the essence of sin. The essence of sin is not acknowledging God's authority as Creator. Once there is sensitivity to a Living God and a sense that Christ reveals that God, we can discuss the blessings and the cost of following Jesus.

Riding the wave

Therefore, rather than fear the modern wave of the authentic self, why not ride the wave? Introducing Christ in terms of identity moves us out of the arena of personal attack and political debate. For so many who don't understand or even know the Bible, it takes us back to a more New Testament style of evangelism. A simple way to introduce the gospel today might begin with something like this: *Society calls us to define who we are; Christ calls us to discover who we are in him.* It would be hard to find a more concise and contemporary summary of human lostness and the impact of saving grace, paving the way to explain who Jesus is and what he did.

Please make no mistake: apart from the Holy Spirit's gracious work, this will sound as foolish today as it did in the first century.[5] Such an approach is not more convincing but may be more understandable. It introduces the gospel to the biblically naive as the Apostles initially did, not as a debate over this or that behavior, but rather in terms of what human beings are relative to the Living God we were created to model.

The problem

There is just one problem with beginning a gospel conversation by discussing our identity. Christians—and I'm thinking of fellow evangelicals in particular—are experiencing an immense identity crisis of our own. The 2022 survey, *The State of Theology* found that among self-identified evangelicals, 48% believe that all major religions worship the same God,

---

[5] 1 Corinthians 1:23.

30% believe Jesus was a great teacher but not God, and 32% believe that religious belief is a matter of opinion as opposed to objective truth.[6] These trends are rising.

And orthodox doctrine isn't the only issue. Peter tells us that while accurate knowledge is essential, following Jesus is mostly about character and relationships or obedience and love. Unfortunately, our constant cultural tension enhances our sensitivity to the other side's sins while obscuring sensitivity to those of our side. As a result, the unity of the Church is fractured, and what it means to follow Jesus is confused.

Sadly, this evangelical identity crisis is becoming harder for the Church to fix because the study mentioned above reveals that more than a quarter of evangelicals feel no obligation to join a church. This means the Church is losing the cultural right to define what it means to be Christian.

At a time when obsession over identity has opened a door for the gospel, Christians barely know who they are.

An opportunity for evangelism

Peter's summary of how to find our identity in Jesus prepares us for gospel ministry in our age. This kind of discipleship should prepare us to open a gospel discussion with any family member, friend, or neighbor who is proudly gay or stands tall as a White supremacist. With either of them and anyone in between, I agree that what we see as right and wrong depends on how we understand ourselves. So let's talk about how we can understand who we are.

Begin by asking them to tell the story behind their choices. Who were the most important influences in their life? What were their significant milestones? What lifestyle decisions have they made, and why? What part of their story is understandable because I have experienced something similar? What is hard for me to understand, and I need them to explain further? I must be patient and compassionate, for

---

[6] *The State of Theology* is a joint study of Ligonier Ministries and LifeWay Research conducted every two years, https://thestateoftheology.com.

honest human stories always include pain and confusion (including mine).

Then I can share that I want my choices rooted in my decision to follow Jesus Christ. That statement alone may sound holier than thou, so I must illustrate with one of the personal stories connected with Peter's Principles, one that seems appropriate to the particular conversation. I might describe how I became aware of my need to know God and what drew me to see God in Jesus. Or what inspired me to want to be like him more than anything. Or something from God's Word that opened my eyes to a new way of looking at life. Or the excitement of experiencing something good that was entirely new to my experience just because Jesus asked me to risk it. Or the powerful resources Jesus provided to free me of something that had sapped my soul. Or a surprising way that God became more real to me in one of his many roles. Or how God opened my heart to recognize radically different people as part of my spiritual family. Or how the Lord helped me overcome my prejudice, so I can care for people who don't share my faith but whom I realize are just as significant as I am.

This approach reserves debates over behavior for later and begins with finding identity in Christ.

"What do you think of gay marriage?"

"Well, that could not be an option for me because I'm a follower of Jesus."

At this point, the discussion moves from personal preference and political pressure to how we make sense of our lives. Homegrown militia members are not the only ones trying to find their place in a world of threats. Transexuals are not the only ones seeking to find their authentic selves. That's what every Christian disciple is doing, too. That's what I'm doing. The difference is that instead of picking through social and personal confusion to find myself, I'm discovering who I am in Christ. I see God in him; therefore, he is my template for being human. His cross and resurrection covered my failures and created a new life for me.

If following Jesus sounds like something they'd like to explore, the door is open for the whole gospel message. If they are not interested, it will not merely be because of a behavioral choice or ideology but because they are determined to live on their own terms, a choice they must defend on the Day of Judgment. Either way, I will try to do them good and honestly model Jesus for as long as we both draw breath.

An opportunity for witness

We need ways of talking about Jesus that take advantage of today's desperate search for identity. But words only go so far. Our witness is also needed. Peter's list reminds us that the fruit of ministry grows out of Jesus' character and love. Yes, we know Jesus through words, but in every genuine Christian, he is also a living presence. Discipleship must be more than teaching Christians how to talk about Jesus.

Consider these thoughts from John Stott:

When we meet some people we know immediately and instinctively that they are different. We are anxious to learn their secret. It is not the way they dress or talk or behave, although it influences these things. It is not that they have affixed a name tag to themselves and proclaimed themselves the adherent of a particular religion or ideology. It's not even that they have a strict moral code which they faithfully follow. It is that they know Jesus Christ, and that he is a living reality to them. They dwell in him and he dwells in them. He is the source of their life and it shows in everything they do.

Not merely in the words you say,
Not only in your deeds confessed,
But in the most unconscious way
Is Christ expressed.

Is it a beatific smile?
A holy light upon your brow?
Oh no! I felt his presence
When you laughed just now.

To me, 'twas not the truth you taught,
To you so clear, to me still dim,
But when you came you brought
A sense of him.

And from your eyes he beckons me
And from your heart his love is shed,
Till I lose sight of you and see
The Christ instead.

These people have an inner serenity which adversity cannot disturb; it is the peace of Christ. They have a spiritual power that physical weakness cannot destroy; it is the power of Christ. They have a hidden vitality that even the process of dying and death cannot quench; it is the life of Christ.

To use Biblical expressions, "The peace of Christ rules in their hearts," "the power of Christ is made perfect in their weakness," and "the life of Christ is made manifest in their mortal flesh."[7]

Stott described what discipleship should prepare us to become. Peter became this kind of person because Jesus is real, alive, and living in his disciples. It is what all Christians should be, and any Christian can be. The lost person trying to find their significance needs to see such Christians. Yes, they need biblical truth and intelligent explanations. But they also need—and in the beginning, need more than anything—the recognizable presence of Jesus Christ.

§

---

[7] This address was given in 1983 at the Leadership Luncheon following the National Prayer Breakfast in Washington, D.C.

The quote is from an article that originally appeared in the Summer 2007 issue of *Knowing & Doing,* part of the C.S. Lewis Institute, used by permission.

There is nothing magical about this approach to evangelism. Christ's gospel of the kingdom will still seem foolish until family, friends, and neighbors gain eyes that see and ears that hear. But when people tire of pinball bouncing off this or that movement, motto, sexual option, conspiracy theory, and social post, they will have heard of an alternative journey with Christ and seen someone on that path. And those who seek the kingdom of God will know where to find the gate.

Peter's Principles tell us how to discover who we are meant to be. If we adopt them for our journey, God will reshape us around the best person who ever lived. In addition to providing a manual on bearing fruit, they also give us a tool to evangelistically engage anyone who, like you and I, searches for their authentic self.

Discussion Questions for Chapter 14

1. Do you find it difficult to talk to people who justify sinful choices by claiming the right to define who they are?
   a) Are we ever tempted to do something similar?
2. How did the Apostles begin the gospel differently with Gentiles as opposed to Jews?
   a) Discuss exploring the gospel with people today who have little biblical knowledge or commitment.
3. What do you think of the idea of sharing the gospel message in concert with a personal witness that can personally illustrate all the various steps of Peter's Principles?
4. Have you ever known someone who brought a sense of Jesus' presence?

Chapter 15: Peter's Principles and the Cultural Mandate

> His divine power has granted to us all things that pertain to life and godliness, through the knowledge of him who called us to his own glory and excellence, by which he has granted to us his precious and very great promises, so that through them you may become partakers of the divine nature, having escaped from the corruption that is in the world because of sinful desire. (2 Peter 1:3-4)

America is in an ongoing struggle for power to control the direction of our culture. The battlefield is everywhere: political campaigns, news reporting, social media algorithms, and school lesson plans. Not since the Civil War has there been so much division, anger, and fear. Social influencers and their followers grasp every conceivable advantage to energize their point of view.

Followers of Jesus are also interested in cultural change, though our Lord inspires different motives and values. Consider the Lord's warning to Israel as they prepared to build a new society amid other nations:

> ... take care that you be not ensnared to follow them ... and that you do not inquire about their gods, saying, "How did

these nations serve their gods?—that I also may do the same." (Deuteronomy 12:29-30)

Followers of the Lord Jesus are forbidden to build God's kingdom with the same agenda and values as the nations we live in. Our objectives will overlap, and we will deal with many of the same matters—a healthy environment, local zoning, national security threats, child abuse, punishment of criminals, competing interests in outer space, and many other public concerns. But Jesus' disciples have a unique goal: to manifest the nature and glory of God. Christians want to make differences in society that reflect the righteousness and compassion of Jesus and, therefore, make life better for everyone.

People try to gain power in lots of ways to change the culture. How should Christians understand our source of power? This question takes us back to the beginning of Peter's Principles:

His divine power has granted to us all things that pertain to life and godliness. (2 Peter 1:3)

Peter says that God promises to give power through the knowledge of Christ that enables his people to escape the corruption in the world and partake of the divine nature.[1] Our Heavenly Father empowered Jesus' ministry through the Holy Spirit when the Eternal Son humbled himself in his incarnation and lived among us with perfect character and love.[2] God will give us similar fruit as we walk with the same Holy Spirit to follow his Son and become like him. In other words, if Christians want divine power to influence our society, we must *first* develop Christ's character and love.

Christ-likeness not only empowers the Great Commission; it also empowers the Cultural Mandate.

---

[1] 2 Peter 1:3-4.

[2] Luke 3:21;4:1; John 3:5-6; Hebrews 9:13-14.

The healing and disruptive power of Christian faith

The Christ-likeness of God's people always brings healing to people around us and naturally shakes society to produce cultural change.

There are many examples of this throughout history. The first occurred during Paul's work in Ephesus.[3] As Paul patiently explained the message of Jesus in the city, the citizens of Ephesus witnessed extraordinary acts of God's power to physically and spiritually heal in Jesus' name. That combination of word and deed resulted in many people turning to Christ from the local idols. Chief among those idols was Artemis, the patron goddess of Ephesus, whose temple was a tourist magnet for religious festivals. There was a lucrative business for silver shrines to the goddess—or, at least, there had been before people turned to Christ. The distraught silversmiths instituted a city-wide riot against the Christian faith, inadvertently demonstrating faith's power to change society without even trying. That is to say, Paul did not preach against the silversmiths or attempt to boycott them. Instead, he preached Christ, and people lost interest in idols. The result was that many Ephesians began to look for civic answers from a rational and compassionate God instead of praying to a meteorite.[4]

The early church demonstrated how increasing Christ-likeness in an increasing number of people had a powerful impact on society. The effect was caused by character changes among Christians rather than through political force. In other words, the transforming Church influenced society as the number of Christians grew and they appealed to the general conscience.

---

[3] Acts 19.

[4] The worship of meteorites was a feature of Greek worship. The original cult object in Ephesus disappeared, but later reconstructions of the temple suggest a meteorite origin.

Tim Keller listed five qualities of the early church that had a remarkable cultural impact:[5]

1. Multi-ethnicity
2. Care for the poor and marginalized
3. Commitment to non-retaliatory forgiveness
4. Strongly and passionately active in response to abortion and infanticide
5. A revolutionized [i.e., biblical] sex ethic

We observed the importance of the first three points when following Peter's discipleship, and I assumed the fifth point in the previous chapter on evangelism. History teaches that these five ethical qualities were historically linked to the early church's impact on society. The early transformation of the character and relationships of Christ's followers left a significant impression on Western civilization.

Other striking historical examples include Celtic Christianity's positive preservation of Western civilization through the early Middle Ages, the faith-based worldview necessary for the development of modern science, the vast strides in government, communication, political freedom, economics, and the dignity of the individual stemming from the Protestant Reformation, the anti-slavery impact of the Clapham Sect and American abolitionists, and many local changes from various revivals. American traditions of caring for the needy, balanced constitutional government, health care, expanding civil freedoms, and higher education all had Christian roots.

It's also true that Christian institutions have been responsible for much social evil in multiple times and ways. However, that evil has been a departure from the commands and teaching of Jesus instigated by spiritually ignorant or corrupt leaders pursuing some kingdom of their own design.

---

[5] *How to Reach the West Again*, Tim Keller, Redeemer City to City, 2020, pp. 25-37.

When many ordinary Christians become increasingly like Jesus Christ, their surrounding society benefits.

Peter's Principles and the power to benefit society

In the examples related to Keller's list, Christians had a substantial social impact because of their Christ-likeness, not clever manipulation of political techniques. In each case, the early church did not jump straight from faith to seeking change in their larger society. First, they added obedience and love to their faith. Cross-cultural respect, compassion, forgiveness, valuing life, and honoring the family were not what the early church *stood for*; they were what the early church *was*. That aroma of Christ often offended people in power but irresistibly attracted many others.[6] With the early Christians, the power to shape society flowed from the power of the Holy Spirit to shape them.

We have seen that this is precisely what Peter teaches. God's power, not only in the Great Commission but also in the Cultural Mandate, begins with saving faith. Then, over four steps, God's power shapes Christian character. Then, over three more steps, God's power uses that character to establish love in our relationships. The order of those last three relationships is critical. Only when changes in our lifestyle enable us to love God and the larger Church will we be able to take *agape* love to the general culture.

The social issues that Christians initially faced are again issues today. Christian involvement in the machinery of our culture may be necessary, but it is not sufficient to make a large difference. Cultural change begins when many individual Christians obey Jesus by changing how we live to escape the corruption of sin and cultivate one-way love. If we skip this step and try to encourage social change in ways we have not personally experienced, there is no divine power.

And Peter says that individually transformed Christians are still not enough to spread the aroma of Christ in our

---

[6] 2 Corinthians 2:14-16.

society. That will also require a similar transformation in Church fellowship. A neighbor or friend may be impacted by the striking lifestyle of a single Christian, but society needs to see a Christian community displaying Christ's character and love within itself. The breadth of our witness in any culture will be no larger than the breadth of our brotherly affection among believers in that culture.

The inference from Peter's Principles is clear. Christians must develop the character to love like Jesus, first privately and then among ourselves, *before* we can expect God's power to help our neighbors flourish.

This is not how today's Christians have been discipled. Instead of doing the work of adding to our faith, we are often satisfied with how God's forgiveness overlooks our sins. Of course, that is true; more than that, it is fundamental. But emphasizing *only* that implies that Christ cannot transform us, and we have nothing valuable to offer when dealing with society's challenges except forgiveness for failure. Praise God for forgiveness! But we who know Christ are called to be living witnesses to his resurrection through his powerful and growing influence within and between us. This is not only essential for divine power in the Great Commission, but it is also equally critical for the Cultural Mandate.

Christians who are moved by our culture's disintegration and want to do something about it cannot limit our response to manipulating the fallen world's government and social institutions. If we want God's power for life and godliness, Peter tells us that we must make every effort to add to our faith and personally produce the fruit that God loves and the world needs to see. Imagine the implications if we had practiced this kind of discipleship when Christian influence was massive in America. Imagine, for example, the flow of our history if most Christian slave-holders had treated their many Christian slaves as full brothers, as Paul exhorted Philemon.[7] Or imagine most American churches offering a safe and

---

[7] See the New Testament Book of Philemon.

supportive home for Christians struggling with sexual confusion, temptation, and failure.

We need a discipleship based on Peter's Principles if we are to benefit society because our influence will not come from what we stand for as much as from who we are. Leaders and members alike will need to stretch their faith to learn new forms of obedience to Christ and then work that obedience into a lifestyle of worship, fellowship, and one-way love for everyone.

§

At this point, let's take a breath. It's vital to remember that transforming our culture is not the main reason we pursue spiritual transformation. Instead, we seek change in ourselves and the Church when that's what is required to follow Jesus. Working on character and love is working on the vineyard. The good works of evangelism and cultural flourishing are the fruit that then comes naturally. Our impact on society will be a newly discovered aspect of who we were meant to be in Christ.

Discussion Questions for Chapter 15

1. What forces do you think are driving cultural change today?
   a) Why do you think Christian influence has declined so much?
2. Look at Keller's five traits of the early church that impacted Western Civilization. Pick one that you think is weaker in today's Church.
   a) In that context, discuss the difference between Christians standing for something and being something.
3. Imagine how some aspect of American history might have been different if the large majority of Christians had obeyed Christ and loved like him at the time.
4. How would you like to see Christ-likeness in the Church impact culture today?

Chapter 16: Summary

Therefore I intend always to remind you of these qualities,
though you know them and are established in the truth that
you have. I think it right, as long as I am in this body, to stir
you up by way of reminder, since I know that the putting off
of my body will be soon, as our Lord Jesus Christ made
clear to me. And I will make every effort so that after my
departure you may be able at any time to recall these things.
(2 Peter 1:12-15)

The Apostle Peter captured the cadence of his journey with
Jesus in seven ordered steps. They describe how Jesus
discipled and taught him how to live in the eternal kingdom of
God that is breaking into the world today. In the above quote
that follows what we've studied, Peter says this list of steps is
his legacy to the Church—something he especially wanted us
to remember after he left for Heaven.

I think Peter was concerned that the Church would forget
that the initial grace to believe in Jesus also enables us to
follow him very much as Peter did. Jesus never meant for faith
in him to be a single religious experience or limited to
religious life. Religion helps us understand, practice, and
celebrate our journey with Jesus, but that journey doesn't
travel on the same broad road as everyone else except for
religious rest stops. Our path may pass through the same
times, places, and roles, but it is different because we get to

travel alongside the risen Jesus with him in the lead. Christians should see themselves as Jesus' disciples, linked to him by the Holy Spirit as Christ continues to bring his kingdom into the world.

But we do not know how to follow Jesus when we come to faith. Peter didn't. Like him, we must be taught. We must be trained—not trained all at once in everything we will ever learn, but trained in how to learn over the rest of our lives. Peter's seven steps provide a framework for reliably and consistently abiding in Christ. When faithfully applied, they activate God's promises to empower our transformation.

The seven steps are simple enough, but they can be further reduced to two profound principles that should guide every discipleship effort. Let's consider each one separately, working backward to appreciate their relationship and then putting them together in their proper order to reveal the entire flow of God's transforming power.

1. Christ's work in me empowers Christ's work through me

Current discipleship tends to focus on ministry, which occurs in the relationships we find toward the end of Peter's list. For example, prayer training explores praise (God), petition (church family), and intercession for our lost world (everyone). Evangelism delights in gospel grace (God), stimulates believers to share it (church family), and practices effective sharing techniques (everyone). All ministry takes place in relationships. This is where Christians want to go— expanding the kingdom of God into the lives of others.

However, a weakness in this approach becomes apparent when we review how Jesus taught Peter to bear fruit. We train Christians for ministry in our relationships but spend little effort training for character development within ourselves. We assume we can manifest Christ's love in ministry to God, the Church, and our neighbors by jumping directly from grace. As a result, the character needed to obey God and cultivate one-way love is assumed or overlooked. Rarely do we find practical training to develop aspiration or help to turn biblical insights into new patterns of personal behavior. Perhaps we believe that virtues like humility, generosity, gentleness, honesty, sexual purity, and contentedness would be nice but aren't necessary to expand God's kingdom. Indeed, too many Christian leaders believed that God would bless their ministry if their character deficiencies were hidden.

But ministry expresses Christ's love, and Peter learned that Christ's love is built with Christ's character. For example, look at the way Peter approaches how any Christian can share the gospel:

> Now who is there to harm you if you are zealous for what is good? But even if you should suffer for righteousness' sake, you will be blessed. Have no fear of them, nor be troubled, but in your hearts honor Christ the Lord as holy, always being prepared to make a defense to anyone who asks you for a reason for the hope that is in you; yet do it with gentleness and respect, having a good conscience, so that, when you are slandered, those who revile your good behavior in Christ may be put to shame. (1 Peter 3:13-16)

Peter says that sharing the gospel (an aspect of ministry) must be in the context of Christ-like character (a good conscience) and Christ-like love (gentleness and respect even toward those who slander us). Sharing the gospel message without these things would demonstrate a lack of honor for Christ. Our evangelism will either honor or dishonor Jesus according to the observable witness of our character and the one-way love it generates.

This may be hard for us to appreciate because we are naturally blind to the assortment of cultural sins which have shaped us and do not realize how much they undermine our witness. We are tempted to think God is automatically pleased when we simply do the right ministry tasks, such as prayer, helping the poor, and evangelism. That is what the Pharisees believed. They imagined God's kingdom as something they could build outside of themselves through exactly those means: prayer, helping the poor, and evangelism.[1] Jesus said that the Pharisees were spiritually blind; they were satisfied with their religious efforts and were unaware of the sin that compromised their impact.[2] When we skip over the character steps of Peter's Principles, we *cannot* replicate the love that empowers ministry. We can only create nice-looking but loveless actions that do not honor Christ.

As a disciple, I must learn early on that God's power does not leap from faith to ministry without changing me first. I must learn to cultivate the aspiration for virtue. I must learn to delight in biblical illumination. I must learn to trust what God says and obey him in ways that counter the sin that has shaped me. I must be eager to change my lifestyle from the one I inherited, believing that Jesus leads me to something better. In other words, I must walk in God's kingdom myself before expecting others to want to join me. Otherwise, I recommend a path that I am not willing to travel—not much of a recommendation.

One common failing of apprentices in any field is assuming the role of an expert too soon, thinking they can lead others like masters without needing to practice first. Disciples of Jesus do that when they attempt to build Christ's kingdom in the world before the Holy Spirit has constructed much of it inside them. That kind of ministry has only the world's motives, understanding, methods, and limitations to work with. When this is how we approach discipleship, it encourages the bad habit of representing to others a Christ we barely know.

My point is not that we must become fully mature before we can represent Christ. My point is that we must be spiritually alive and growing to represent the Living God. Through his teaching and example, Peter shows that aspirational, divinely instructed, steadfast obedience to God is the potent witness of Christ's character that empowers the

---

[1] Matthew 6:2-6, 23:15.
[2] Matthew 15:10-20

loving work of kingdom expansion through all our relationships.

Christ's work in me empowers Christ's work through me.

2. Christ's work for me empowers Christ's work in me.

Love for God and others is the overflow of growing obedience to God. Working backward, that kind of character also must arise from somewhere.

The bad news is that my sin compromised my motives for Christ-like character. Pride, guilt, shame, the desire to please—none of these motives can stimulate genuine obedience to God from the heart. I spent so long twisting my character around the fallen world that obeying Jesus became foreign to who I was.

But the good news is that Jesus changed who I am! Faith in Christ signals that God the Father has attributed the character and love of his Son to me, and the Holy Spirit has already recreated the core of my being in the likeness of Jesus.[3] Through faith, God has made me a new creation.[4] Whenever I make an effort to build on that faith, I discover a little more of the new me.

> If then you have been raised with Christ, seek the things that are above, where Christ is, seated at the right hand of God. Set your minds on things that are above, not on things that are on earth. For you have died, and your life is hidden with Christ in God. When Christ who is your life appears, then you also will appear with him in glory.
>
> Put to death, therefore what is earthly in you: sexual immorality, impurity, passion, evil desire, and covetousness, which is idolatry. On account of these the wrath of God is coming. In these you too once walked, when you were living in them. But now you must put them all away ... seeing that *you have put off the old self with its practices and have put on the new self, which is being renewed in knowledge after*

---

[3] John 3:3-8; Titus 3:3-7.

[4] 2 Corinthians 5:17.

the image of its creator. (Colossians 3:1-10, *emphasis added*)

Through his saving work for us and the gift of his Spirit in us, Jesus gives us new selves! This is not something we could have done or would have done. He did it for us.

Jesus's work for us is why we are allowed to follow him, want to follow him, and can follow him with increasing success. Simple faith that this is true saves us. We never leave that faith behind to move on to other things. Instead, everything we build must rest upon it. Whenever that faith is active, and we work to add to it, we experience more of the new person we have already become.

Christ's work for me empowers Christ's work in me.

§

Putting it all together

Peter was determined that we remember how Jesus can transform any disciple. God's power flows through Christ to create a new and godly identity that mirrors the divine nature we see in Jesus. The Holy Spirit works with us to manage that power through a sequence of seven qualities.

- The simplified schematic: Christ's work for me empowers Christ's work in me, which empowers Christ's work through me.
- The full design specs for following Jesus: add to faith virtue, to virtue knowledge, to knowledge self-control, to self-control steadfastness, to steadfastness godliness, to godliness brotherly affection, and to brotherly affection love.

When these qualities are all present, working together, and increasing, fruit grows all by itself, and kingdom expansion is *inevitable.*

§

Jesus changed Simon's life not by forcing an unnatural lifestyle but by changing his identity. Simon found God in Jesus before he could explain it theologically. As Jesus cultivated character and love within his disciple, Simon found himself living in the kingdom of God. With Jesus, he learned that God thought of him not as a sinner but as an adopted son with Jesus' credentials, privileges, and responsibilities. The more Christ's Spirit worked within him, the more Jesus' purpose became his purpose, Jesus' hopes and plans became his hopes and plans, and Jesus' mission became his mission. He was the prototype Christian disciple.

The change did not happen overnight. He may not even have noticed when Jesus began calling him Peter more often than Simon, but as Jesus showed him the person God designed him to be, the new name stuck. After all, we haven't been studying the Book of 2 Simon.

Discovering our new identity in Christ is the result of following Jesus. It isn't pretense, and the change isn't even hard. Change comes all by itself when we diligently work on seven qualities in the way Peter taught us. They describe what it means to abide in Christ.

What I find most encouraging is that spiritual growth need not follow The Peter Principle and plateau when our faith runs into an obstacle. Instead, Peter's Principles enable growth in any circumstance and at any age, connecting us to the Holy Spirit's power whenever we add to our faith. Peter's simple, profound, and comprehensive guide to discovering ourselves in Christ is an outstanding pattern for discipleship—a final contribution from the Rock of Daniel's prophecy, a fisherman whose faith signaled the arrival of God's kingdom in Jesus.

Discussion Questions for Chapter 16

1. What sorts of things come to mind when you think of the word "legacy"?
    a) Why do you think Peter thought of the seven steps as his legacy?
2. Unpack these summary statements:
    a) Christ's work for me empowers Christ's work in me.
    b) Christ's work in me empowers Christ's work through me.
3. Discuss the statement: "Jesus changed Simon's life not by forcing an unnatural lifestyle but by changing his identity."

Chapter 17: Applications

The close of this study brings us to the question of how to use 2 Peter 1:3-8 in practical discipleship. I encourage every reader to join me in exploring new ways to apply Peter's teaching. Here are six suggestions to get the ball rolling:

1. Think of discipleship as an apprenticeship in following Jesus

I believe Peter's Principles correct two erroneous concepts of what discipleship is meant to be. The first understands discipleship as a concise course typically including a basic doctrinal overview, an introduction to spiritual disciplines like prayer, Bible study, and witnessing, an explanation of Christian life concepts, and perhaps something about commitment to the Church. Once you've mastered the content, you may be encouraged to immediately become a disciple-maker by leading others through the same material.

This approach misunderstands discipleship by confusing it with an introduction to Christianity. Such introductions are quite helpful, but they are not discipleship. Discipleship is about following Jesus. The Christian faith is designed to help us do that, but many adhere to the religion without following Christ in any perceptible way.[1] Discipleship is about faith

---

[1] Matthew 7:21-27.

overflowing in a desire for moral goodness, searching for knowledge, offering new obedience, and reshaping one's lifestyle around God, Christ's Church, and our neighbors. It's about becoming like Jesus Christ and finding our place in his mission. Discipleship should focus on actually *doing* these things—taking the first steps to build a life with Christ instead of only discussing religious concepts.

The other error confuses discipleship with our entire spiritual journey. Mature Christians understand there is always more to Jesus, always more of God's love, righteousness, holiness, and mercy to learn and enjoy. Because our sin is so pervasive, there is always more freedom to experience. Following Jesus is, as Eugene Peterson memorably described it, "a long obedience in the same direction."[2]

But to call our entire spiritual journey discipleship loses the term's original sense of an initial apprenticeship. We travel best when we understand up front where we are going. People often come to Christ for good personal reasons without being taught God's reason for saving them. What has God called us to be and do? How has he made his power available to achieve our calling? Believers who are never trained in these things have only their natural motives, strength, and understanding to draw upon. They are forced to teach themselves what to do with all the religion they will consume over the years.

Jesus' call is indeed vast, and our journey will be extensive. By including the command "teaching them to obey all I have commanded" in the Great Commission, following Jesus embraces the entire Cultural Mandate. Following Jesus brings God's kingdom into us and extends it through us in every relationship as we join Jesus in his mission. The life of a disciple is, indeed, a long obedience.

Discipleship, however, does not describe a disciple's entire life but rather preparation for how to live it. Discipleship is not meant to train a disciple in everything, just as the Naval Academy does not graduate Admirals. Christians will spend a

---

[2] *A Long Obedience in the Same Direction: Discipleship in an Instant Society,* Eugene Peterson, IVP, 2019.

lifetime growing in the Body of Christ.[3] Discipleship gets us started by teaching what Jesus' calling is and how to effectively pursue it from *faith* to *character* to *love* and into *mission*. Discipleship is only the beginning of a disciple's journey, but a good start can make that journey epic.

Let's reinstitute an apprenticeship in following Jesus.

2. Teach disciples to see Jesus in themselves

Peter teaches how believers can find their true identity in Jesus. This is the essence of discipleship.

Churches arising from the Reformation have developed a strong tradition that appreciates what it means to be "in Christ." We saw this in Chapter 5 on faith, where we looked at Peter's introduction in 2 Peter 1:1. I am saved not by my righteousness but by the righteousness of Christ attributed to me. Jesus and I exchange reputations so that Jesus bore my sin on the cross, and I wear Jesus' righteousness that raises me to sit at the Father's right hand. Jesus is sitting there, and I am in him.[4] This truth concerns my position in Christ, how God accepts me, and the basis for my eternal hope. We cannot stress this too much.

But my union with Christ also goes in the other direction. Not only am I in Christ, but Christ is in me:

> I have been crucified with Christ. It is no longer I who live, but Christ who lives in me. And the life I now live in the flesh I live by faith in the Son of God, who loved me and gave himself for me. (Galatians 2:20)

The Holy Spirit extends God's kingdom into my life by causing my heart, my inner being, to come alive to God.[5] My new heart exercises saving faith, but that is not all. It is also the beginning of a new me because the seed of Christ's nature has been planted within.[6] I need training to identify with my new

---

[3] Ephesians 4:11-16.

[4] Colossians 3:1-3.

[5] Jeremiah 31:31-35; Ezekiel 36:24-27; John 3:3-6.

[6] 1 Peter 1:23; 1 John 3:9.

nature because I cannot become like Christ while clinging to the old one.

> We know that our old self was crucified with him in order that the body of sin might be brought to nothing, so that we would no longer be enslaved to sin ...
> So you also must consider yourselves dead to sin and alive to God in Christ Jesus. (Romans 6:6-11)

If we see ourselves as the same sinners we always were, we will continue to find our identity in our old values and habits. Christ's goodness will feel alien to us, and we'll keep it at arm's length. We will confess sin as what we really want instead of what God says we ought to want. We will ask God to change our old nature into something better. This approach does not work because our old nature is unchangeably hostile to God and unable to transform.[7]

Instead, we must exercise faith that through Christ, God created a new heart within us.[8] This seed of our new nature trusts God, wants to leave sin behind, and yearns to be like Jesus. Christians must be trained to regularly exercise faith that God has *already* changed them down deep, for it is only the new nature that can grow and bear fruit. We still confess sin, but see it as something alien to what we want most down deep. We thank God for already giving us a new heart and ask for strength to expand its influence to overcome old habits that no longer suit who we now are.

Peter described how to do this in seven steps, but the Apostle Paul captured the essence of it with a powerful image. He recalled how Moses' face shined with God's glory—so much so that he felt compelled to wear a veil.[9] Paul compared that with how the Holy Spirit enables any believer in Christ to see God's glory *in their own face*. He used the idea of a mirror to explain:

---

[7] Romans 8:7.

[8] Ezekiel 36:25-27; Jeremiah 31:31-34; Hebrews 8:8-12.

[9] Exodus 34:29-35.

> But we all, with unveiled faces, looking as in a mirror at the glory of the Lord, are being transformed into the same image from glory to glory, just as from the Lord, the Spirit. (2 Corinthians 3:18, NASV)

When I look in a mirror, I naturally see myself. But when the Holy Spirit removes the veil or opens my eyes, I can look in a mirror and see *Jesus*—glorious Jesus in me. By faith, I can see his purity, compassion, and righteousness within me whether or not I feel it at the moment and even if I only see it dimly.[10] I affirm by faith that the sinful desires still echoing inside me no longer reflect the new person Christ has created.[11] Peter's Principles teach me how to supplement my faith to uncover my new nature even as my mortally wounded old nature continues to spasm. The more clearly I see Jesus in me when I look in the mirror, the more I transform into the same image from glory to glory. In other words, the identity change accomplished by the Holy Spirit on the inside causes transformation that God's holy commandments never could from the outside.[12]

Christians often think spiritual growth means struggling with God as if he were pressing unwanted holiness upon us. Recalling that Christ lives in me sweeps away that lie. God desires to strive *together with me* against sinful habits that neither of us wants and no longer reflect the new person God has created.[13] Disciples must be taught to repeatedly exercise faith that God is no longer their Judge; he is now their Friend and Helper who lives in them through the Holy Spirit. Spiritual growth happens when I stop trying to change an old corrupt nature that is dying and start discovering a new Christ-like nature that's already alive.

---

[10] 1 Corinthians 13:12.

[11] Romans 7:14-20.

[12] Romans 8:1-16.

[13] 2 Corinthians 5:17.

Disciples need to learn that our union with Christ not only saves us; it defines who we now are and what we are becoming.

3. Focus on character and love

The Great Commission (which includes the Cultural Mandate) was Jesus' last command to his disciples—not the first. Peter said that he especially wanted us to remember how Jesus taught him that kingdom fruitfulness is the result of cultivating character and love.

Contemporary discipleship tends to be impatient to press believers into ministry, especially seeking to lead others to Christ. Of course, it makes sense to help new believers thoughtfully summarize the gospel and their witness since they want to share their faith with loved ones and must be ready to explain the changes others see.

But if we press believers to expand God's kingdom without prioritizing the growth of Christ-likeness within themselves, their effort will lack what it needs to be effective. This is because proclaiming the good news of God's kingdom requires a recognizable reflection of it in us. If our efforts to expand God's kingdom around us are detached from the Holy Spirit's expansion of God's kingdom in us, our evangelism will lack a compelling witness. This is how evangelism turns into an intellectual debate or sales program instead of good news about how others can share the life they see in us.[14] Christians do not need to become mature in the faith before they share the gospel, but they should genuinely illustrate something of the moral and relational transformation that shows what faith in Christ looks like.

Peter taught us the flow of spiritual growth that every disciple needs to learn. Discipleship should prepare us for a faith journey that pursues character, the love that character generates, and the mission that love compels.

---

[14] Compare 1 Peter 3:15-16 with 2 Corinthians 2:17.

4. Integrate direct experience

A spiritual apprenticeship should be approached as Jesus did by mixing instruction with guided practice. If discipleship is to concentrate on character and love, we need to practice incorporating lifestyle changes.

Let's add projects that give hands-on experience transitioning between Peter's seven qualities. Like a shop class assignment to build a birdhouse I may never use, such training projects may seem artificial, but they give believers a taste of God's power, moving them from faith to love. Imagine discipleship participants completing real-world projects that demonstrate they can:

a) privately celebrate gospel grace to inspire their desire to be like Jesus.

b) on their own, learn something about a topic in the Bible.

c) experiment with new obedience directed by what they learned from the Bible.

d) allow others to help them turn some new obedience into an ongoing lifestyle change, and then specifically do so in the following three areas ...

e) modify a personal habit around one of God's roles.

f) treat a Christian who is not currently their friend as their family.

g) contribute to good works or gospel communication directed to non-Christians.

Such projects need only demonstrate an introductory competence with the seven qualities. It doesn't matter how simple or easy these projects are, so long as disciples complete them with supervised feedback. For example, I could learn something new from the Bible (b) by journalling one week with a recommended devotional and meditating on one relevant verse. I could experience fellowship beyond my friends (f) by visiting an elderly church member for coffee and trading life stories. I could invest in disaster relief or missions (g) by contributing money to an appropriate organization, carefully praying through one of their newsletters, and introducing their work to someone else.

Is this as far as they ever take their faith? No. Peter promises that we will advance further and further over time, and the more we grow, the more our ministry will naturally develop. While we should not experience swimming for the first time through a high dive into the deep end, we do need to get wet and learn how to float in the shallow end. New Christians need a first taste of God's power as they apply obedience to relationships. Experienced Christians also need this wherever they still lack experience with a particular step or transition between steps. When they finish their introductory projects, they will have modest but genuine stories about how they have followed Jesus and will have developed a taste for more.

If disciples learn to accomplish small things, they will eventually do great things.[15]

5. Use Peter's Principles wherever we can

Peter explained how we can work with the Holy Spirit to manage the flow of God's transforming power and discover who God designed us to be. The goal of discipleship is to provide every new believer with initial training in how God's power flows from faith through obedience to relationships and, finally, through our relationships into ministry.

But initial training has little value if we do not regularly practice. It may be helpful to occasionally rehearse Peter's sequence in common forms of training like new member classes or leadership preparation. More useful would be to regularly apply it in specific scenarios:

Personal devotions. Quiet time with God is an opportunity to renew our faith and get fresh direction. Peter's sequenced qualities are like a gentle path up a hill with seven overlooks to view one's life. There's always a good place to appreciate

[15] John 14:12.

where we have traveled already and where the Holy Spirit would take us next.

Personal growth is almost always blocked by some inability to move from one step to the next in a specific area of life. Peter shows us how that blockage affects all the steps that come after. Even better, he enables us to trace back to what may be responsible for that particular weakness. It's like fixing a wet basement. Instead of mopping it out every time it rains, we would do better to repair cracks in the walls or direct drainage away from the house, going back from effect to cause until we find the real problem. Peter's Principles help us understand ourselves and how spiritual growth works.

Counseling. Counselors come alongside us when we experience a fracture in our soul or within a relationship. Peter's Principles assist counselors by pointing to Scripture for the knowledge of life's design, tracing the path of character development, and demonstrating how our relationships are related and layered. Most importantly, they stress the fundamental need for an open-hearted embrace of God's grace. This is because insights into God's intention for my life are only compelling when linked to a new identity in Christ that motivates me to live like him.

As with personal devotions, Peter's Principles also give counselors an effective diagnostic of spiritual, character, and relationship issues by helping them discover where the power of God's grace is blocked. The presenting problem may be at one step, but the underlying issue may relate to a previous one.

Leadership. From prayer to programs to training, spiritual leaders seek God's transforming grace in themselves, their congregation, and their community. They aren't just interested in activities, numbers, and fame. They want divine power to manifest Jesus to the glory of God. Peter tells us how to work with the Holy Spirit to accomplish this, and the principles are as helpful for a congregation as they are for an individual. Rather than focus exclusively on building ministries, Peter encourages us to prioritize the more challenging work of leading worship that promotes aspiration, uprooting the common cultural sins that have shaped us, and broadening the range of our fellowship. Doing that will allow God's power to flow into ministry unrestricted.

Peter's Principles help leaders plan for the experiences their congregation needs. While churches typically understand spiritual growth and ministry in terms of some or all of Peter's steps, Peter's Principles add the insight that growth occurs in the *transitions* between the steps as each supplements the previous one. This suggests that leaders create regular opportunities for members to gain guided experience with each transition.

Evangelism. Jesus understood the gospel in terms of the kingdom of God, and so should we.[16] Peter's seven steps are an honest travel brochure of what God's kingdom is like. The gospel should not only include directions to the gate but also explain and demonstrate life on the other side. From faith to character to relationships to ministry, Peter outlines where Jesus would take us. The great doctrine of justification answers how sinners can get into God's kingdom, but it's only an answer for someone seeking to come in.

Let's make Peter's Principles a much-used item in our toolbox.

6. Follow those who are already following Jesus

Peter learned from Jesus' example as well as his teaching. Since he shared so much of his story in the New Testament, it would seem that making disciples involves personally demonstrating the character, love, and mission we wish others to learn.[17] Peter's Principles give substance to Paul's invitation: "Be imitators of me, as I am of Christ."[18] Those being discipled need a leader's example.

---

[16] Mark 1:14-15, and many, many references to the kingdom in Jesus' teaching.

[17] Matthew 10:24-25.

[18] 1 Corinthians 11:1.

Finally, brothers, whatever is true, whatever is honorable, whatever is just, whatever is pure, whatever is lovely, whatever is commendable, if there is any excellence, if there is anything worthy of praise, think about these things. What you have learned and received and heard and seen in me—practice these things, and the God of peace will be with you. (Philippians 4:8-9)

Remember your leaders, those who spoke to you the word of God. Consider the outcome of their way of life, and imitate their faith. (Hebrews 13:7)

Looking at these verses, note how we are told to imitate our leaders. When Paul urged us in the Book of Philippians to practice what we see in him, he was not talking about evangelism, prayer, or planting churches. Instead, he referred to truth, honor, justice, purity, and whatever is lovely, commendable, excellent, and worthy.[19] Likewise, when the Book of Hebrews cited what we should imitate, it referred not to our leaders' preaching but to their way of life.

This means disciple-making does not require mentors to reproduce their ministry in others. There are as many different ways to build God's kingdom as there are parts of the body.[20] Christians being discipled need not mirror their mentors' ministry choices, and mentors ought not to imply that they should. Disciple-making leaders use their stories as examples of a journey that follows Jesus, not as standards for everyone's ministry.

The need for examples does not imply that we need perfect discipleship trainers. Consider how the stories of so many biblical figures—Peter especially—teach by illustrating failure as well as success. We simply need disciple-makers with recognizable experience in developing the steadfast character and one-way love of Jesus Christ and who have followed that love to find their role in Christ's mission. Their journey doesn't have to sound impressive as long as it is authentic.

---

[19] Philippians 4:8-9.
[20] 1 Corinthians 12:1-30.

I remember two men I knew as a college student in 1970. One was a professional house painter my fellowship group chanced upon during a summer evangelism project in Philadelphia. A magnetic leader, he spoke freely of Christ and offered to help us financially by subcontracting some of his work. He was inspiring as he brought younger men under his wing, casting a vision of spiritual power and economic success. However, halfway through a summer of hard labor, our less-than-minimum-wage results were torpedoing our hopes for college funds. Then one of his devoted proteges let it slip that the reason for our poor pay was that our fearless leader had been specifically told by God to "see his world" and needed to accumulate money for extensive travel! Quitting that job (followed by the rest of the team) was the hardest thing I had yet done. Respectfully going up against his powerful personality was daunting, and I had no idea how to meet my college expenses. (What the Lord did to provide for us over the second half of that summer was truly astonishing —another story I like to tell).

In the fall, I returned to my physics studies at the University of Maryland, where I met with another man, John. He was an officer assigned to the Pentagon who quietly participated in our fellowship retreats and other special events. Occasionally, he would show up for most of a weekday and make himself available without any agenda. He would support us in sharing the gospel with other students or spend time discussing aspects of our walk with Christ. We could discuss anything. I learned from what he said, from his questions, by watching how he treated people with respect and how he discretely used his money to build Christ's kingdom. It was so natural that I didn't realize I was being discipled.

I later learned the secret of John's occasional weekday appearances: he could take time off when he gave blood. He literally gave his blood to be there for us—for me. As I write this, that was over fifty years ago. I hope to speak with John next week by phone. These days, we connect every two weeks to keep encouraging each other's faith.

Another of my earliest mentors, Graham, says every spiritual advance is usually associated with a person. Besides John and Graham, people I have followed include shepherds Bill Mahlow, Allen Harris, and Paul Quinn, teachers R. C. Sproul, Barbara Boyd, Roger Nicole, and Elizabeth Elliot, and some I only encountered through their writing like C. S. Lewis, John Stott, Francis Shaeffer, and A. W. Tozer. While at seminary, Billy Graham shared personal accounts of his journey that I needed to hear. When I mention Billy Graham, you know who I'm talking about, but there are others I have imitated whose names few would know, though God does. All these men and women shared their history of experiencing Jesus' resurrection power on a journey from faith through character and love to find a place in Christ's mission.[21]

I have tried to follow them as they followed Jesus—not becoming any of them but reflecting Christ as the person God designed me to be. My story may not sound impressive, but it has been authentic.

§

After studying a draft of Peter's Principles, a new friend, Claude, remarked that his spiritual journey had been a challenging jigsaw puzzle. Sections of it made sense, but he always felt he was missing the box cover showing how the whole thing fits together. He said that reviewing Peter's discipleship overview gave him that picture. I think that's exactly what Peter was trying to do.

This study suggests an approach to discipleship that, in some respects, differs from what we are used to. Contemporary discipleship programs are some of the best teaching and training available, but the Church needs more and needs it now. I ask everyone committed to discipleship to find better ways to integrate what the Apostle Peter said about how to follow Jesus.

---

[21] Ephesians 1:15-21.

Discussion Questions for Chapter 17

1. Do you think today's Christians need an apprenticeship in following Jesus?
2. Discuss the distinction between faith that I am in Christ and faith that Christ is in me.
3. How can believers best be prepared to expand the kingdom of God in others?
4. Do you think discipleship needs practical projects to assist in learning?
5. How might Peter's Principles be integrated into our whole Christian experience?
6. What would you most want to be true of someone who is discipling you?

Appendix: The Student, the Fish, and Agassiz

The Student, the Fish, and Agassiz[1]
by the Student [Samuel H. Scudder]

It was more than fifteen years ago that I entered the laboratory of Professor Agassiz, and told him I had enrolled my name in the scientific school as a student of natural history. He asked me a few questions about my object in coming, my antecedents generally, the mode in which I afterwards proposed to use the knowledge I might acquire, and finally, whether I wished to study any special branch. To the latter I replied that while I wished to be well grounded in all departments of zoology, I purposed to devote myself specially to insects.

"When do you wish to begin?" he asked.

"Now," I replied.

This seemed to please him, and with an energetic "Very well," he reached from a shelf a huge jar of specimens in yellow alcohol.

---

[1] *American Poems, 3rd ed.*, Boston: Houghton, Osgood & Co., 1879, pp. 450-54. (Also, it's easy to find on the internet.)

"Take this fish," he said, "and look at it; we call it a Haemulon; by and by I will ask what you have seen."

With that he left me, but in a moment returned with explicit instructions as to the care of the object entrusted to me.

"No man is fit to be a naturalist," said he, "who does not know how to take care of specimens."

I was to keep the fish before me in a tin tray, and occasionally moisten the surface with alcohol from the jar, always taking care to replace the stopper tightly. Those were not the days of ground glass stoppers, and elegantly shaped exhibition jars; all the old students will recall the huge, neckless glass bottles with their leaky, wax-besmeared corks, half-eaten by insects and begrimed with cellar dust. Entomology was a cleaner science than ichthyology, but the example of the professor who had unhesitatingly plunged to the bottom of the jar to produce the fish was infectious; and though this alcohol had "a very ancient and fish-like smell," I really dared not show any aversion within these sacred precincts, and treated the alcohol as though it were pure water. Still I was conscious of a passing feeling of disappointment, for gazing at a fish did not commend itself to an ardent entomologist. My friends at home, too, were annoyed, when they discovered that no amount of eau de cologne would drown the perfume which haunted me like a shadow.

In ten minutes I had seen all that could be seen in that fish, and started in search of the professor, who had, however, left the museum; and when I returned, after lingering over some of the odd animals stored in the upper apartment, my specimen was dry all over. I dashed the fluid over the fish as if to resuscitate it from a fainting-fit, and looked with anxiety for a return of a normal, sloppy appearance. This little excitement over, nothing was to be done but return to a steadfast gaze at my mute companion. Half an hour passed, an hour, another hour; the fish began to look loathsome. I turned it over and around; looked it in the face -- ghastly; from behind, beneath, above, sideways, at a three-quarters view -- just as ghastly. I was in despair; at an early hour, I concluded that lunch was necessary; so with infinite relief, the fish was carefully replaced in the jar, and for an hour I was free.

On my return, I learned that Professor Agassiz had been at the museum, but had gone and would not return for several hours. My fellow students were too busy to be disturbed by continued conversation. Slowly I drew forth that hideous fish, and with a feeling of desperation again looked at it. I might not use a magnifying glass; instruments of all kinds were interdicted. My two hands, my two eyes, and the fish; it seemed a most limited field. I pushed my fingers down its throat to see how sharp its teeth were. I began to count the scales in the different rows until I was convinced that that was nonsense. At last a happy thought struck me -- I would draw the fish; and now with surprise I began to discover new features in the creature. Just then the professor returned.

"That is right," said he, "a pencil is one of the best eyes. I am glad to notice, too, that you keep your specimen wet and your bottle corked."

With these encouraging words he added --

"Well, what is it like?"

He listened attentively to my brief rehearsal of the structure of parts whose names were still unknown to me; the fringed gill-arches and movable operculum; the pores of the head, fleshly lips, and lidless eyes; the lateral line, the spinous fin, and forked tail; the compressed and arched body. When I had finished, he waited as if expecting more, and then, with an air of disappointment:

"You have not looked very carefully; why," he continued, more earnestly, "you haven't seen one of the most conspicuous features of the animal, which is as plainly before your eyes as the fish itself. Look again; look again!" And he left me to my misery.

I was piqued; I was mortified. Still more of that wretched fish? But now I set myself to the task with a will, and discovered one new thing after another, until I saw how just the professor's criticism had been. The afternoon passed quickly, and when, towards its close, the professor inquired,

"Do you see it yet?"

"No," I replied. "I am certain I do not, but I see how little I saw before."

"That is next best," said he earnestly, "but I won't hear you now; put away your fish and go home; perhaps you will be ready with a better answer in the morning. I will examine you before you look at the fish."

This was disconcerting; not only must I think of my fish all night, studying, without the object before me, what this unknown but most visible feature might be, but also, without reviewing my new discoveries, I must give an exact account of them the next day. I had a bad memory; so I walked home by Charles River in a distracted state, with my two perplexities.

The cordial greeting from the professor the next morning was reassuring; here was a man who seemed to be quite as anxious as I that I should see for myself what he saw.

"Do you perhaps mean," I asked, "that the fish has symmetrical sides with paired organs?"

His thoroughly pleased, "Of course, of course!" repaid the wakeful hours of the previous night. After he had discoursed most happily and enthusiastically -- as he always did -- upon the importance of this point, I ventured to ask what I should do next.

"Oh, look at your fish!" he said, and left me again to my own devices. In a little more than an hour he returned and heard my new catalogue.

"That is good, that is good!" he repeated, "but that is not all; go on." And so for three long days, he placed that fish before my eyes, forbidding me to look at anything else, or to use any artificial aid. "Look, look, look," was his repeated injunction.

This was the best entomological lesson I ever had -- a lesson whose influence was extended to the details of every subsequent study; a legacy the professor has left to me, as he left it to many others, of inestimable value, which we could not buy, with which we cannot part.

A year afterwards, some of us were amusing ourselves with chalking outlandish beasts upon the blackboard. We drew prancing star-fishes; frogs in mortal combat; hydro-headed worms; stately craw-fishes, standing on their tails, bearing aloft umbrellas; and grotesque fishes, with gaping mouths and staring eyes. The professor came in shortly after, and was as much amused as any at our experiments. He looked at the fishes.

"Haemulons, every one of them," he said; "Mr. _____ drew them."

True; and to this day, if I attempt a fish, I can draw nothing but Haemulons.

The fourth day a second fish of the same group was placed beside the first, and I was bidden to point out the resemblances and differences between the two; another and another followed, until the entire family lay before me, and a whole legion of jars covered the table and surrounding shelves; the odor had become a pleasant perfume; and even now, the sight of an old six-inch worm-eaten cork brings fragrant memories!

The whole group of Haemulons was thus brought into review; and whether engaged upon the dissection of the internal organs, preparation and examination of the bony framework, or the description of the various parts, Agassiz's training in the method of observing facts in their orderly arrangement, was ever accompanied by the urgent exhortation not to be content with them.

"Facts are stupid things," he would say, "until brought into connection with some general law."

At the end of eight months, it was almost with reluctance that I left these friends and turned to insects; but what I gained by this outside experience has been of greater value than years of later investigation in my favorite groups.

About the Author

Dr. Glenn Parkinson has been learning and preaching the Bible for over 40 years. Converted while completing his undergraduate degree in physics, Glenn's goal is to discover the themes and patterns that weave God's Word into a meaningful and beautiful whole. As a Reformed Pastor (now Emeritus) with a professional doctorate from Westminster Theological Seminary, he believes that truth is the engine for living in ways that glorify, enjoy, and please the Lord.

Glenn lives with his wife and best friend, Micki, and a cat that constantly battles the computer for attention.

All of Glenn's books are available on Amazon, and you can contact him through www.growthground.org.

Glenn's books include, in order of when they were written:

Like the Stars - a Christian alternative to culture war

Should Christians be fighting a "culture war?" Seven key Bible insights outline how evangelicals can recapture their potential to enrich life in America.

Share Your Master's Joy - a partnership that lasts forever

Stewardship is finding joy in managing all of life to God's glory. Such joy pleases the Lord and directs his choice of future leaders.

Living Faith - convictions that bring faith to life

A faith to live by requires convictions rooted in God's Word. Here are fourteen powerful convictions, each illustrated by a character study from the Bible.

Tapestry - the Book of Revelation

The Book of Revelation was never meant to be a puzzle. The greatest challenge is not understanding it but rather believing it shows us the real world as God sees it. When we see the world as God does, the most important thing in life becomes crystal clear.

A Larger Faith - the Book of Daniel

The Book of Daniel does more than simply demonstrate faith. By documenting a series of extraordinary predictive visions given to Daniel, it describes the worldview that naturally enlarges faith among God's people.

Peter's Principles - learning to follow Jesus

In his last recorded letter to the Church, the Apostle Peter highlighted a peculiar list of seven qualities that summarize how Jesus discipled him. Peter said they are the key to experiencing the power of God as we discover the person God designed each of us to be.

Made in the USA
Middletown, DE
03 November 2023

41727505R00146